DANIEL'S

ENTERTAINING AT
HOME WITH A
FOUR-STAR CHEF

DISH

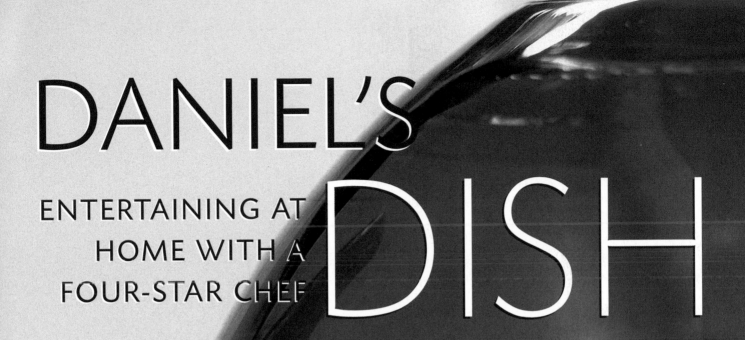

DANIEL'S

ENTERTAINING AT HOME WITH A FOUR-STAR CHEF

DISH

DANIEL BOULUD

PHOTOGRAPHS BY PETER MEDILEK

ELLE DECOR

filipacchi
publishing

To Micky and Alix for whom I cook Daniel's dishes at home.

Food stylists, Cyrille Allannic,
Rémy Fünfrock and Lior Lev Sercarz

Designer, Patricia Fabricant
Prop stylist, Sonja Jurgens
Editor, Jessica Dheere
Copyeditor, Jennifer Ditsler-Ladonne

Photographs copyright © Peter Medilek /
Food Look NYC

First published in the United States of America by
Filipacchi Publishing
1633 Broadway
New York, NY 10019

Includes index

ISBN 2-85018-662-7

Printed in Italy

Contents

6   Foreword by Margaret Russell

8   Introduction

10   Cocktails, Small Bites, and Starters

60   Fish and Shellfish

90   Meat, Poultry, and Side Dishes

122   Breads and Desserts

168   Menus for Entertaining

170   Seasonal Menus

172   Pantry Basics

173   Basic Equipment for the Kitchen

174   Kitchen Source Guide

176   Credits

178   Tableware Source Guide

179   Behind the Scenes

180   Acknowledgments

181   Index by Season

183   Index of Wines and Spirits

185   Index of Recipes and Ingredients

Foreword

by Margaret Russell

I'm fairly certain that when Daniel Boulud asked me to write the foreword to this book, he was under the impression that I could cook. After all, we'd known each other even before he began writing "Daniel's Dish" for ELLE DECOR in 1995. Over the years, we've spent a lot of time together—planning the columns for the magazine at his three Manhattan restaurants, DANIEL, Café Boulud and DB Bistro Moderne; and at charity fundraisers and ELLE DECOR events. But somehow the subject of my kitchen skills never came up. Thankfully, he was unaware that the contents of my refrigerator consisted of champagne, bottled water, mustard, jam, and a few jars of Crème de la Mer moisturizer.

And, yes, to tell the truth, I had often collaborated with one of the greatest chefs of our time and hadn't even attempted to whip up a single one of the recipes he'd created for the magazine. I had every intention of doing so, of course, but a litany of excuses prevented me—I travel a great deal, I work late hours, it's so much easier to order in or eat out, and so on. After my initial reluctance (and panic that my complete lack of interest in turning on an oven would finally be revealed), I had an epiphany: I love a great meal, I enjoy entertaining and I have, in fact, cooked in the past and could conceivably try it once again.

So I started by refamiliarizing myself with my kitchen appliances and taking baby steps—family dishes from childhood and recipes from magazines, newspapers, and cookbooks. To lower my anxiety level, I avoided any recipes with more than six ingredients. I made many mistakes: I couldn't tell the difference between scallions and leeks, I stubbornly refused to follow directions, and I burned food I didn't even know could burn. But as my confidence grew and my culinary skills advanced, the process of cooking at home began to give me more pleasure than pain; it ceased to be intimidating and was actually fun. Amazingly, by the time I received the advance material for this cookbook, I was even ready to attempt Daniel's Carrot Mirror Tart on page 32. (Although it requires more than six ingredients, it's relatively easy and, better yet, it looks impressive!)

Both novice and gourmet cooks will appreciate the uncomplicated approach of *Daniel's Dish: Entertaining at Home with a Four-Star Chef*. It's rare for a world-class chef to produce a guide for the home cook that isn't too daunting, but, like Daniel himself, this book is straightforward and pragmatic. More than just a compilation of the best of Daniel's ELLE DECOR columns from the past eight years, it features both newly created dishes and updates of perennial favorites. Recipes for everything from frozen drinks and canapés to cassoulet and spicy sea bass to cupcakes and cherry clafoutis are organized into four sections, followed by suggested menus for entertaining as well as menus based on the availability of seasonal ingredients. Wine pairings for each dish are also provided, thanks to the expertise of restaurant DANIEL's award-winning sommelier, Jean Luc Le Dû, whose taste and insight have always been an integral part of the "Daniel's Dish" columns. The book even includes a shortlist of pantry essentials (my kitchen is now well stocked), basic equipment every home chef should own, and Daniel's topflight sources for tableware and kitchen products.

Readers who have had the memorable experience of dining at one of Daniel's four restaurants (Café Boulud in Palm Beach opened last summer) will recognize his trademarks: extraordinary attention to detail, a focus on fresh seasonal ingredients of the highest quality, a constant quest for a surprising mix of flavors, and subtle sophistication without an ounce of pretense. *Daniel's Dish*, like ELLE DECOR, celebrates passion, joie de vivre, and inspiration from around the globe, and encourages the reader to experiment and play.

As for me, my neighborhood bistro is off my speed dial and I'm no longer apoplectic at the thought of cooking a holiday turkey—proof that there's no one better than Daniel Boulud to show us all that, like decorating, cooking and entertaining with style should be easy, relaxing, and fun.

Margaret Russell, ELLE DECOR's editor-in-chief

Introduction

Dinner service is the point at which the curtain rises at my restaurant DANIEL. The day's preparation—the baking of breads and pastries, the selection of ingredients, the polishing of silver and arranging of flowers, the finalizing of the menu—is complete, and the guests start to arrive. The maître d's, waiters, sous-chefs, line cooks, and busboys, like the cast of an opera, have taken their places and are waiting for their cue to begin.

My desire, always, is that, in the execution of their individual roles, the members of my staff make everyone feel as if the entire production has been orchestrated just for them. From that touch of crème fraîche gently applied to a caviar canapé with a single fork tine to the light and airy spun-sugar basket of a Pineapple and Coconut Givré, every detail should reinforce the idea that an evening at DANIEL is nothing short of a dream.

I can't imagine the host who wouldn't want this, even on a small scale, for his guests. What host doesn't want to serve a beautifully concocted cocktail? What cook wouldn't relish an "It smells wonderful!" from a special friend? And what amateur pastry chef wouldn't want their table companions to gasp like children as the desserts exit the kitchen? This impulse to please strikes me as similar to that which inspires designers and homeowners to realize their singular visions for the interiors published in ELLE DECOR, which is why eight years ago, when my recipes began to run in the magazine, the partnership seemed so natural.

Recreating such a scene may sound like a daunting task, especially for the home chef, but it is far from an impossible one. With the recipes here, as with the ones that have appeared in ELLE DECOR, I share my style of home entertaining, giving readers insight into how I prepare meals for friends and family—the people I most love to cook for. I want to convey that with planning, fresh seasonal ingredients, and simplified techniques, the home kitchen can become a source of dishes that reveal the depth of flavor and surprising juxtapositions of textures that guests have come to expect at my restaurants. Equally important is to make sure that cooks using these recipes can also enjoy the time they have with their guests, as I do during dinner service at DANIEL, so particular attention has been paid to allowing for preparation in stages and keeping last-minute steps to a minimum. Most of all, I want to give you the tools and techniques that will let you enjoy the chef's art as much as I do.

Many of the ELLE DECOR dishes resurface here, but a number of the recipes represent new creations or, in a few cases, adaptations of longtime favorites, like the Asian-, North African-, and Indian-inspired renditions of my Classic Burger. Divided into four chapters—Cocktails, Small Bites, and Starters; Fish and Shellfish; Meat, Poultry, and Side Dishes; and Breads and Desserts—*Daniel's Dish* ranges from traditional European country fare to American recipes that take a global approach to cuisine. Accompanying every dish is also a suggestion for a complementary wine from my sommelier Jean Luc Le Dû. Whatever the dish, you can be certain it was conceived as a celebration of the season, and whatever

the celebration, you can be just as sure you'll find a fitting dish.

As you read through the following pages with thoughts of assembling that perfect menu, I challenge you to adopt the spirit of both of my restaurants and ELLE DECOR and reinterpret the recipes according to your own tastes. Substitute ingredients and revise techniques. If you can't find morels, replace them with another mushroom. If you prefer a vegetarian version of the Curried Tuna–Stuffed Radishes, try shredded crudités. Don't shy away from a recipe because you don't have a specific piece of equipment. Soups and sauces can be strained through cheesecloth or a knitted kitchen towel instead of a fine-mesh sieve, for example. In short, don't be afraid to take risks, because in the same way that ELLE DECOR might move its readers to build a beautiful kitchen, I want to encourage you to use yours.

DANIEL BOULUD, 2003

Cocktails, Small Bites, and Starters

Nothing erases the to-do lists of the day like cocktail hour, when something as simple as a bite-size Parmesan basket filled with goat cheese and a glass of dry Spanish wine—and perhaps a little flamenco music—are all you need to relax. It's a time for experimentation, for mixing new drinks, trying out an unexpected dish or two, and devising menus that play with the contrasts between tastes and textures.

One of the best things about cocktail hour is that it provides home chefs with the opportunity to use their creativity to set the mood for an entire evening. For instance, a bamboo-leaf-lined platter of Chicken Satay served with minty mojitos can turn any summer evening into a tropical escape, while a strawberry-infused Berrini paire

with Curried Tuna-Stuffed Radishes could be just right for pretheater hors d'oeuvres. Hosting a supper-like party that requires more substantial fare may call for Smoked-Salmon Potato Latkes or a Provence-inspired Mediterranean Tart, even as a sophisticated luncheon may demand the Waldorf Moderne. And of course, when a touch of elegance is in order, there's always Blini with Caviar and Crème Fraîche.

Whatever you choose to prepare, the canapés, appetizers, and soups presented here can certainly help you get the night off to a good start. Above all, though, make sure to plan ahead, because the most important part of the evening won't be spent in the kitchen but in the company of family and friends.

Berrini

Makes 1 cup of syrup

2 pints ripe strawberries, hulled and quartered
½ cup sugar
½ cup tightly packed fresh mint leaves

Combine the strawberries and sugar in a large bowl, cover with plastic wrap, and let macerate in the refrigerator for 48 hours, stirring once or twice a day.

Line a large sieve with a triple layer of cheesecloth and set over a large bowl.

Pour the strawberry mixture into a medium saucepan, add the mint leaves, and bring to a boil. Lower the heat and simmer for 3 minutes. Transfer to the sieve. Refrigerate overnight to allow the syrup to drain into the bowl. *(The syrup will keep for at least 2 weeks when stored in an airtight container in the refrigerator.)*

For each Berrini, gently stir 1 to 2 tablespoons of the fruit syrup into a glass of champagne, white wine, or sparkling water.

Crème Boulud

Makes 4 servings

2 large egg yolks
1½ cups heavy cream
½ vanilla bean, split and scraped
¼ cup sugar
2 Tbsp praline paste (available at specialty
    markets)
1 Tbsp cognac or brandy
2 Tbsp Frangelico liqueur
Ice cubes for serving

Prepare an ice-water bath in a large bowl. Whisk together the egg yolks, 1 cup of the heavy cream, vanilla-bean seeds and pod, and sugar in a small saucepan. Cook over medium heat, stirring constantly with a wooden spoon, until the mixture thickens enough to coat the back of the spoon or reaches 180°F on an instant-read thermometer, 3 to 4 minutes. Strain through a fine-mesh sieve into a medium bowl. Place the bowl in the ice-water bath and cool completely.

Combine the custard, the remaining ½ cup heavy cream, praline paste, cognac, and Frangelico in a blender and puree until smooth. Put ice cubes into four glasses and add the crème. Serve immediately.

Daniel's Mojito

Makes 4 servings

½ cup sugar
½ cup freshly squeezed lime juice
1 bunch mint, leaves only
¼ cup plus 1 Tbsp light rum
1 tsp unflavored gelatin

Bring the sugar and ½ cup water to a boil in a small saucepan; stir until the sugar has dissolved. Let cool.

Stir the lime juice into ½ cup of the sugar syrup. Pour into a metal loaf pan and place in the freezer. Stir periodically with a fork, until the mixture is frozen and granular, 2 to 3 hours.

Prepare an ice-water bath in a small bowl. Bring a small saucepan of water to a boil. Add the mint leaves and blanch until tender, 2 to 3 minutes. Drain the leaves and add to the ice-water. Let cool and drain again. Squeeze the leaves to remove any excess water.

Combine the blanched mint leaves, rum, and remaining sugar syrup in a blender and puree until smooth.

Sprinkle the gelatin over 1 tablespoon cold water in a cup; let soften for 5 minutes.

Warm the gelatin and ¼ cup of the rum-mint mixture in a small saucepan just until the gelatin has dissolved. Stir in the remaining rum-mint mixture. Pour into four champagne flutes so that each is about one-third full and refrigerate until barely set, about 30 minutes. Top with the lime granité and add light rum to taste. Stir before drinking.

Frozen Seabreeze

Makes 4 servings

¼ cup sugar
1 cup cranberry juice
1 cup fresh or frozen cranberries
½ cup Absolut Citron vodka, plus more
    for serving
Freshly squeezed juice of ¼ lemon
1 cup freshly squeezed grapefruit juice

Bring the sugar and ¼ cup water to a boil in a small saucepan; stir until the sugar has dissolved. Let cool.

Combine the cranberry juice and cranberries in a blender and puree until smooth. Strain through a fine-mesh sieve into a metal loaf pan. Stir in 2 tablespoons of the sugar syrup and put the pan in the freezer. Stir periodically with a fork, until the mixture is frozen and granular, 2 to 3 hours.

Meanwhile, stir together 1 cup water, the vodka, 4½ tablespoons of the sugar syrup, and the lemon juice. Pour into a separate metal loaf pan and put in the freezer. Stir periodically with a fork, until the mixture is frozen and granular, 2 to 3 hours.

Stir together the grapefruit juice and the remaining 2 tablespoons sugar syrup. Pour the liquid into a third metal loaf pan and put in the freezer. Stir periodically with a fork, until the mixture is frozen and granular, 2 to 3 hours.

To Serve
Spoon a layer of cranberry granité into four 8-ounce martini glasses. Next, add a layer of the vodka granité. Finish with a layer of grapefruit granité. Top with Absolut Citron to taste. Stir before drinking.

Parmesan Baskets

with Herbed Goat Cheese

Makes about 40 hors d'oeuvres

1½ cups finely grated fresh Parmesan cheese
6 ounces fresh goat cheese, softened
¼ cup milk
1 large shallot, finely chopped
2 Tbsp finely chopped mixed fresh herbs, such as
    chives, cilantro, flat-leaf parsley, and tarragon
1 Tbsp extra-virgin olive oil
1 tsp sherry vinegar
Salt and freshly ground white pepper
Assorted nuts, cut into small pieces, or fresh herbs

Center a rack in the oven and preheat to 350°F. Have at least 2 empty egg cartons on hand.

Place a 1½- to 2-inch cake ring on a nonstick baking sheet and fill, with a thin even layer (no more than ⅛ inch thick) of Parmesan cheese. Carefully lift the ring without disturbing the cheese. Repeat to make 11 more cheese rounds, spaced 1 inch apart. (If not using a mold, the shape can be improvised.)

Bake for 4 to 5 minutes, making sure they don't overbrown, until bubbly and lightly golden brown. Using a small offset spatula, quickly and carefully lift the hot Parmesan rounds, one by one, off the baking sheet and gently press into the egg-carton divots. It is easiest to shape the baskets when hot. Repeat with the remaining cheese. *(Once cool, the Parmesan baskets can be kept overnight in an airtight container in a cool, dry place. If it is humid, however, they are best served the same day.)*

Mix together the goat cheese, milk, shallot, herbs, olive oil, and sherry vinegar in a medium bowl, and season with salt and pepper.

Transfer the goat-cheese mixture to a piping bag and pipe into the baskets, or fill them using two small spoons. Garnish each basket with a nut or fresh herb.

A dry wine from the Rueda region of Spain—from the Basa winery, for example—would make a great complement to the crunchy yet creamy Parmesan baskets. Not only will the wine's fruit flavors contrast with the slight earthiness of the canapés, but its mineral quality will bring out the flavor of the goat-cheese filling.

Baked Littleneck Clams

with Prosciutto

Makes 36 hors d'oeuvres

1 medium tomato
1 medium red bell pepper
1 Tbsp extra-virgin olive oil
3 Tbsp finely chopped shallots
2 sprigs sage, leaves finely chopped
1 Tbsp finely chopped flat-leaf parsley leaves
2 slices prosciutto, finely chopped
½ cup fresh bread crumbs
8 Tbsp (1 stick) unsalted butter, cut into pieces,
    at room temperature
5 drops Tabasco
Salt and freshly ground pepper
36 littleneck clams, shucked, shells reserved
Seaweed for garnish

Preheat the broiler.

Bring a small pot of water to a boil. Cut a small X in the base of the tomato and lower it into the boiling water. Blanch for 25 to 30 seconds. Drain and run under cold water. When cool, peel, seed, and finely chop. Set aside.

Place the red pepper on the rack of a broiler pan. Broil as close as possible to the heat, turning every 5 minutes, until the skin is blistered and charred, 10 to 15 minutes. (Or using a long-handled fork char the pepper over an open flame, turning it until the skin is blackened, 2 to 3 minutes). Transfer the pepper to a bowl, cover, and let steam until cool enough to handle. Peel, cut off the top, and discard the seeds and ribs; finely chop.

Warm the olive oil in a small skillet over medium heat. Add the shallots and cook, stirring, until translucent. Add the sage, parsley, tomato, and red pepper, and cook 2 to 3 minutes. Drain on a paper-towel-lined plate. Let cool.

Put the vegetables, prosciutto, bread crumbs, butter, and Tabasco in a food processor; season with salt and pepper. Pulse until well blended and crumbly.

Put each clam in a shell half and top evenly with 1 teaspoon of the bread-crumb topping mixture. Arrange the stuffed clams in a jelly-roll pan, and broil, watching closely, until the topping is golden brown, 5 to 7 minutes.

To Serve

Cover a serving tray with seaweed and the reserved clam-shell halves, open side down. Arrange the baked clams on top. Serve hot with small seafood forks or toothpicks.

These clams pack a little heat because of the Tabasco and are best served with a very dry, mineraly wine. The stony quality of Martín Códax's Albarino from Rias Baixas, Spain, offers a nice counterweight to the richness of the dish while its lemony aromas add a touch of freshness.

Curried Tuna–Stuffed Radishes

Makes about 30 hors d'oeuvres

10 to 15 Easter radishes or large red radishes, stems and roots removed

3 Tbsp extra-virgin olive oil

¼ cup minced shallots

⅓ cup diced mango

1 tsp Madras curry powder

⅛ tsp Galanga powder or ground ginger

⅛ tsp ground mace

⅛ tsp turmeric

Pinch of red-pepper flakes

1 Tbsp rice-wine vinegar

½ avocado, peeled and pitted

One 6-ounce can water-packed tuna, drained and flaked

¼ cup chopped celery, plus small leaves for garnish

3 Tbsp diced red apple

3 Tbsp diced Granny Smith apple

3 Tbsp finely chopped unsalted cashews

2 Tbsp freshly squeezed lime juice

1 Tbsp Dijon mustard

1 Tbsp chopped mint leaves

1 Tbsp chopped cilantro leaves

1 Tbsp chopped flat-leaf parsley leaves

1 Tbsp shredded unsweetened coconut

½ Tbsp mayonnaise

¼ tsp finely grated peeled fresh horseradish or ½ tsp bottled horseradish, drained

¼ tsp finely grated peeled ginger

Salt and freshly ground white pepper

Cut 6 to 7 of the radishes into ¼-inch-thick slices. Using a mandoline, very thinly slice the remaining radishes.

Warm the olive oil in a small skillet over low heat. Add the shallots and cook, stirring, until translucent, about 4 minutes. Add the mango, curry, Galanga, mace, turmeric, and red-pepper flakes, and cook, stirring, for 4 minutes. Stir in the vinegar; transfer the mixture to a bowl and let cool.

Using a fork, mash the avocado and add to the mango mixture, along with the tuna, celery, apples, cashews, lime juice, mustard, mint, cilantro, parsley, coconut, mayonnaise, horseradish, and ginger. Combine well and season with salt and pepper.

To Serve

Place 1 teaspoon of the curried tuna in the center of each thick radish slice. Place two thin radish slices, upright on either side of the tuna, edges resting on the radish base. Garnish each with a celery leaf. (*Can be assembled 1 hour ahead and refrigerated.*)

With curry and apple preparations, I love using a Gewurztraminer for its rose petal and spicy qualities. Alsatian versions, while good, can be a little sweet, so it is preferable to seek out the latest vintage of La Cadallora's dry, lean version from the Alto Adige region of Italy.

Blini with Caviar

and Crème Fraîche

Makes about 40 hors d'oeuvres

⅓ cup buckwheat flour
⅓ cup all-purpose flour
Pinch of baking soda
½ cup beer
1 large egg, separated, plus 2 egg whites
1 Tbsp milk
⅛ tsp salt
Vegetable oil or clarified butter
12 ounces caviar
Crème fraîche for serving

Whisk together the buckwheat and all-purpose flours, baking soda, and beer in a large bowl. Let rest for 5 minutes. Whisk in the yolk, milk, and salt. In a separate bowl, whisk the 3 egg whites until stiff peaks form. Fold the beaten whites into the buckwheat batter just until incorporated. Fill a plastic squeeze bottle with a ¼-inch opening with the batter (a spoon can also be used). Stir the batter occasionally.

Warm 1 tablespoon oil or butter in a large nonstick skillet over high heat. When the oil is very hot (it should smoke lightly), squeeze out as many 1½-inch circles of batter as will fit on the pan. When the tops of the blini dry a bit and the bubbles pop, about 2 minutes, flip them over. They should be nicely browned. Cook for 1 minute more to lightly brown the second side. Repeat with the remaining batter, adding oil to the pan as needed. Transfer the blini to a paper-towel-lined plate. Serve while warm. (*The blinis can also be cooled, wrapped by the dozen in plastic wrap, and refrigerated up to 3 days. When ready to serve, rewarm the packets in the microwave.*)

To Serve
Place a dollop of caviar on each blini and garnish with a touch of crème fraîche. Serve immediately.

The neutral character of OP Vodka balances the explosive combination of caviar and crème fraîche. But the truly adventurous may want to try a hollyberry Eau de Vie produced by an Alsatian company called Mette whose floral aromas and dryness add an exotic dimension to the caviar.

Potato Latkes
with Smoked Salmon, Quail Eggs, and Watercress

Makes 40 latkes

20 quail eggs
1½ pounds Yukon Gold potatoes, peeled and
coarsely grated
3 scallions, trimmed and coarsely chopped
2 large eggs, lightly beaten
1 Tbsp finely chopped flat-leaf parsley leaves
1 Tbsp minced chives
Salt and freshly ground pepper
Extra-virgin olive oil
1 cup heavy cream
1 bunch watercress (about 6 ounces), leaves only

Bring a large pot of water to a boil. Prepare an ice-water bath in a large bowl. Gently lower the eggs into the boiling water and cook for exactly 2 minutes. Drain immediately, then transfer the eggs to the ice-water bath. When cooled, drain and carefully peel the eggs. Wrap in plastic and refrigerate.

Squeeze the grated potato with your hands to remove the excess water; place in a medium bowl. Add the scallions, lightly beaten eggs, parsley, and chives; season with salt and pepper; and toss well to combine.

Warm 1 tablespoon olive oil in a large nonstick skillet over high heat. Form latkes that are about 1½ inches in diameter and ¼ inch thick. When the oil is hot, add some latkes to the pan. Cook until golden brown, 3 to 5 minutes, then flip over and cook until crisp and golden brown on the bottom and tender on the inside, another 3 to 5 minutes. Transfer to a paper-towel-lined plate to drain. Repeat with the remaining potato mixture, adding olive oil as needed. Sprinkle with salt and serve immediately, or reheat to serve later.

Bring the heavy cream to a boil in a medium saucepan. Add the watercress and stir until well combined; remove from heat. Puree the heavy-cream-and-watercress mixture in a blender until smooth. Strain through a fine-mesh sieve. Refrigerate until cool.

To Serve
6 ounces sliced smoked salmon, cut into 1-inch
squares
2 Tbsp minced chives

Using a whisk or a mixer fitted with a whisk attachment, whip the watercress cream until it forms soft peaks. Season with salt and pepper. Cut the quail eggs in half lengthwise and place a half on each warm latke. Drape a salmon square around each egg and garnish with a dollop of the watercress cream and a sprinkling of chopped chives. Serve immediately.

A bone-dry Chardonnay from Burgundy such as the Chablis Premier Cru "Montée de Tonnerre" from Louis Michel 2000 (an exceptional vintage) perfectly complements the smoked salmon even as the wine's inherent creamy quality holds its own against the richness of the latkes.

Potato and Reblochon Tart

Makes 6 servings

FOR THE TART SHELL
1 cup plus 3 Tbsp all-purpose flour
6 Tbsp cold unsalted butter, cut into pieces
1/8 tsp salt
1 large egg, lightly beaten

FOR THE FILLING
1¼ pounds Yukon Gold potatoes, peeled and
    cut into ½-inch-thick slices
1¼ to 1½ cups milk
1 cup heavy cream
2 sprigs thyme
2 cloves garlic, lightly crushed
1 Tbsp unsalted butter
1 medium onion, diced into ½-inch cubes
Salt and freshly ground white pepper
1 large egg
¼ tsp freshly grated or ground nutmeg
½ pound Reblochon cheese, rind removed,
    cut into ¼-inch-thick slices

TO MAKE THE TART SHELL
Put the flour, butter, and salt in a food processor and pulse until crumbly. Add the egg and pulse just until moist curds form—don't overprocess. Turn the dough out onto a work surface and knead it once or twice to pull it together. Flatten into a disk, wrap in plastic wrap, and refrigerate for at least 1 hour. *(Wrapped airtight, the dough can be refrigerated for up to 2 days or frozen for up to a month.)*

Place an 8-by-1½-inch cake ring on a parchment-paper-lined baking sheet. Lightly dust a work surface and the top of the dough with flour. Roll the dough out into a round that is about 11 inches in diameter and ⅛ inch thick. As you roll, lift the dough and, if necessary, dust with flour. Fit the dough into the bottom and against the side of the ring, taking care not to stretch it. Trim the excess dough even

with the ring's rim. If the dough cracks, use lightly moistened scraps to fill the cracks. Refrigerate the tart shell for at least 30 minutes.

Center a rack in the oven and preheat to 350°F.

Line the crust with a parchment-paper round and fill with dried beans or rice. Bake for 18 to 20 minutes. Remove the paper and beans, and bake 3 to 5 minutes more, or until lightly colored. Transfer to a rack to cool. *(The crust can be kept at room temperature for up to 8 hours.)*

TO MAKE THE FILLING
Combine the potatoes, 1 cup of the milk, the heavy cream, 1 sprig of thyme, and 1 clove of garlic in a medium saucepan, and season with salt and pepper; bring to a boil. Reduce the heat and simmer until the potatoes are tender, 25 to 30 minutes. Discard the thyme and garlic and let the potatoes cool in the liquid.

Melt the butter in a small skillet over medium-low heat. Add the onion, the remaining sprig of thyme, and the other clove of garlic, and season with salt and pepper. Cook, stirring frequently, until the onions are translucent and tender, 13 to 15 minutes. (Add a tablespoon of water if the skillet gets too dry.) Remove from heat, discard the thyme and garlic and set aside to cool.

Drain the potatoes, straining the milk mixture into a liquid measure. Add enough of the remaining milk to equal 1 cup. Whisk together the egg and nutmeg in a small bowl. Whisk in the milk mixture and season with salt and pepper.

A voluptuous yet crisp and refreshing dry white Alsatian wine will cut through the richness of the tart. Domaine Paul Blanck Gewurtzraminer "Cuvée Classique" 2000 makes a classically styled but powerful counterpart.

Place the tart shell on a parchment-paper-lined baking sheet. Pour half of the filling into the crust. Scatter half of the onions, half of the potatoes, half of the Reblochon on top, then top with the rest of the filling, onions, and Reblochon. Arrange the remaining potatoes in a pinwheel pattern, pressing them into the filling so the custard can bubble up around them. Bake for about 1 hour or until the top has browned and a knife inserted into the center comes out clean. Let cool for 5 minutes before serving.

TO SERVE
Cut the warm tart into 6 wedges and serve with a frisée salad containing chopped crisp bacon, toasted walnuts, and finely chopped shallots. Make a vinaigrette using walnut oil, sherry vinegar, and salt and pepper to dress the salad. Serve an assortment of thinly sliced charcuterie, such as saucisson Lyonnais, prosciutto, bresaola, and chorizo, along with cornichons and pickled onions, to round out the meal.

Mediterranean Tomato–Lemon Tart

Makes 6 servings

FOR THE TART SHELL
1 cup plus 3 Tbsp all-purpose flour
6 Tbsp cold unsalted butter, cut into pieces
Finely grated zest of 1 lemon
⅛ tsp salt
1 large egg, lightly beaten

FOR THE TOMATOES AND THE LEMON CUSTARD
2 Tbsp extra-virgin olive oil
2 cloves garlic, thinly sliced
Leaves from 2 sprigs thyme, chopped
8 plum tomatoes, peeled, halved, and seeded
Salt and freshly ground white pepper
½ cup milk
½ cup heavy cream
2 large eggs
2 large egg yolks
Freshly squeezed juice of 2 lemons
¼ cup Niçoise olives, halved, pitted
2 Tbsp coarsely chopped basil leaves

TO MAKE THE TART SHELL
Put the flour, butter, zest, and salt in a food processor and pulse until crumbly. Add the egg and pulse just until moist curds form—don't overprocess. Turn the dough out onto a work surface and knead it once or twice to pull it together. Flatten it into a disk, wrap in plastic wrap, and refrigerate for at least 1 hour. *(Wrapped airtight, the dough can be refrigerated for up to 2 days or frozen for up to a month.)*

The richness of a Viognier-based wine echoes the flavors of the custard while the grape's floral overtones blend well with the tart's lemony aromas. In particular, a rare Condrieu from the northern Rhône Valley, like the one produced by Tardieu-Laurent, makes a stunning choice. As always with Viognier, get the most recent vintage.

Place an 8-inch tart pan with a removable bottom (or a tart ring) on a parchment-paper-lined baking sheet. Lightly dust a work surface and the top of the dough with flour. Roll the dough out into a round that is about 10 inches in diameter and ⅛ inch thick. As you roll, lift the dough and, if necessary, dust with flour. Fit the dough into the bottom and against the side of the pan, taking care not to stretch it. Trim the excess dough even with the pan's rim. If the dough cracks, use lightly moistened scraps to fill the cracks. Refrigerate the tart shell for at least 30 minutes.

Center a rack in the oven and preheat to 350°F.

Line the crust with a parchment-paper round and fill with dried beans or rice. Bake for 18 to 20 minutes. Remove the paper and beans, and bake 3 to 5 minutes more, or until lightly colored. Transfer to a rack to cool. *(The crust can be kept at room temperature for up to 8 hours.)*

TO MAKE THE FILLING
Reduce the oven temperature to 300°F.

Line a baking sheet with foil, brush with 1 tablespoon of olive oil and sprinkle with the garlic and thyme. Place the tomato halves, cut side down, on the baking sheet, sprinkle with the remaining 1 tablespoon oil, and season with salt and pepper. Bake for approximately 1 hour until the tomatoes are tender but still able to hold their shape; set aside.

Whisk together the milk, cream, eggs, yolks, lemon juice, olives, and basil in a bowl; season with salt and pepper.

Place the tart shell on a parchment-paper-lined baking sheet. Arrange the tomatoes, cut side up, in the tart shell and pour in the custard mixture. Bake 25 to 30 minutes to set. Transfer to a rack to cool.

To Serve
Cut the tart into wedges and serve with summer greens seasoned with a lemon-juice-and-olive-oil dressing.

Carrot Mirror Tart

with Carrot–Coriander Cream

Makes 6 servings

FOR THE TART SHELL
1 cup plus 3 Tbsp all-purpose flour
6 Tbsp cold unsalted butter, cut into pieces
Salt
1 large egg, lightly beaten

FOR THE FILLING
6 medium carrots, trimmed and peeled
½ cup Fontina cheese, in ¼-inch cubes
Pinch of ground cumin
1 cup heavy cream
1⅓ cups carrot juice
3 large egg yolks
Pinch of cayenne
Salt and freshly ground white pepper
3¾ tsp unflavored gelatin

TO MAKE THE TART SHELL

Put the flour, butter, and ⅛ teaspoon salt in a food processor and pulse until crumbly. Add the egg and pulse just until moist curds form—don't over-process. Turn the dough out onto a work surface and knead it once or twice to pull it together. Flatten it into a disk, wrap in plastic wrap, and refrigerate for at least 1 hour. *(Wrapped airtight, the dough can be refrigerated for up to 2 days or frozen for up to a month.)*

Place a 9½-inch tart pan with a removable bottom (or a tart ring) on a parchment-paper-lined baking sheet. Lightly dust a work surface and the top of the dough with flour. Roll the dough out into a circle that is approximately 11 inches in diameter and about ⅛ inch thick. Fit the dough into the bottom and against the side of the pan, taking care not to stretch it. Trim the excess dough so that it is even with the pan's rim. If the dough splits, use lightly moistened scraps to fill the cracks. Refrigerate the tart shell for at least 30 minutes.

Center a rack in the oven and preheat to 350°F.

Line the crust with a parchment-paper round and fill with dried beans or rice. Bake for 18 to 20 minutes. Remove the paper and beans, and bake 3 to 5 minutes more, or until lightly colored. Transfer to a rack to cool. *(The crust can be kept at room temperature for up to 8 hours.)*

To Make the Filling
Reduce the oven temperature to 325°F. Place the tart shell still in its pan on a parchment-paper-lined baking sheet.

Prepare an ice-water bath in a large bowl. Bring a large pot of salted water to a boil, add the carrots and cook until tender, 15 to 20 minutes. Cool in the ice-water bath, drain well, then cut them into 2-by-¼-by-¼-inch sticks.

Arrange half the carrots in tight rows on the bottom of the tart shell; sprinkle half the cheese on top. Arrange the remaining carrots in rows perpendicular to the first layer, top with the remaining cheese, and sprinkle with the cumin.

Whisk together the cream, the ⅓ cup of carrot juice, egg yolks, and cayenne in a bowl. Season with salt and pepper and carefully pour the custard over the filling. Bake for 20 to 25 minutes, until a knife inserted into the center comes out clean. Refrigerate until cool.

Sprinkle the gelatin over ¼ cup cold water in a small saucepan; let soften for 5 minutes. Warm over low heat, stirring, until the gelatin dissolves. Warm the remaining 1 cup of carrot juice and stir it into the gelatin. Season with salt and pepper and set aside. When cool, pour it over the cooled tart to form a thin, even layer. Let set at room temperature.

For the Salad
4 medium carrots, julienned or coarsely grated
1 small bunch cilantro, leaves only
1½ Tbsp extra-virgin olive oil
Freshly squeezed juice of ½ lemon
Salt and freshly ground white pepper

Toss together the carrots, cilantro, olive oil, and lemon juice in a small bowl. Season to taste with salt and pepper.

For the Whipped Cream
½ cup heavy cream
1 Tbsp carrot juice
1 tsp finely chopped cilantro leaves
Pinch of ground cumin
Salt and freshly ground white pepper

Whisk together the heavy cream, carrot juice, cilantro, and cumin in a mixing bowl until soft peaks form. Season with salt and white pepper; refrigerate until ready to serve.

To Serve
Cut the tart into 8 wedges. Serve with the salad and a small dollop of the seasoned whipped cream.

Low in alcohol, a bit sweet, and with a bracing acidity, the 2001 German Riesling Kabinett Trocken "Gimmeldinger Mandelgarten," Müller-Catoir is an appropriate complement, as is the Clos Roche Blanche Touraine Sauvignon 2000, which is mellow, aromatic, fruity, and on the light side.

Four–Greens Tart

Makes 6 servings

For the Tart Shell
1 cup plus 3 Tbsp all-purpose flour
6 Tbsp cold unsalted butter, cut into pieces
⅛ tsp salt
1 large egg, lightly beaten

For the Filling
1 Tbsp extra-virgin olive oil
1 cup finely chopped onion
1 sprig rosemary, leaves only, finely chopped
1 sprig thyme, leaves only, finely chopped
1 clove garlic, finely chopped
Pinch of freshly grated nutmeg
Salt and freshly ground pepper
2¼ pounds spinach, stemmed and washed
½ pound arugula, stemmed and washed
5 ounces dandelion, stemmed and washed
¼ pound watercress, stemmed and washed
3 Tbsp chopped chives
5 sprigs chervil, leaves only, chopped
5 sprigs cilantro, leaves only, chopped
3 sprigs dill, leaves only, chopped
3 sprigs tarragon, leaves only, chopped
3 Tbsp mascarpone cheese
2 Tbsp ricotta cheese
1 cup finely grated fresh Parmesan cheese

To Make the Tart Shell
Put the flour, butter, and salt in a food processor and pulse until crumbly. Add the egg and pulse just until moist curds form—don't overprocess. Turn the dough out onto a work surface and knead it once or twice to pull it together. Flatten it into a disk, wrap in plastic wrap and refrigerate for at least 1 hour. *(Wrapped airtight, the dough can be refrigerated for up to 2 days or frozen for up to a month.)*

Place a 9-by-1½-inch cake ring on a parchment-paper-lined baking sheet. Lightly dust a work surface and the top of the dough with flour. Roll the dough out into a round that is about 11 inches in diameter and ⅛ inch thick. As you roll, lift the dough and, if necessary, dust with flour. Fit the dough into the bottom and against the side of the ring, taking care not to stretch it. Trim the excess dough so that it is even with the ring's rim. If the dough splits, use moistened scraps to fill the cracks. Refrigerate the tart shell for at least 30 minutes.

Center a rack in the oven and preheat to 350°F.

Line the crust with a parchment-paper round and fill with dried beans or rice. Bake for 18 to 20 minutes. Remove the paper and beans, and bake 3 to 5 minutes more, or until lightly colored. Transfer to a rack to cool. *(The crust can be kept at room temperature for up to 8 hours.)*

To Make the Filling
Warm the olive oil in a small skillet over medium heat. Add the onion, rosemary, thyme, garlic, and nutmeg, and season with salt and pepper. Cook while stirring until the onions are translucent, 8 to 10 minutes. Remove from heat and let cool.

Prepare an ice-water bath in a large bowl. Bring a large pot of salted water to a boil. Add the spinach, arugula, dandelion, and watercress and blanch until tender, 3 to 4 minutes. Cool in the ice-water bath, drain well, and squeeze out the excess water. Puree half of the blanched greens, half of the onion mixture, the chives, chervil, cilantro, dill, tarragon, mascarpone, and ricotta in a food processor or blender until smooth. Taste and season with salt and pepper.

Preheat the broiler.

Coarsely chop the remaining greens, mix together with the remaining onion mixture, and season with salt and pepper. Spoon into the bottom of the tart shell, spoon the greens puree on top, and smooth with a spatula. Sprinkle with the Parmesan and broil for 5 minutes. Reduce the oven temperature to 350°F and bake the tart until the top is golden brown, 10 to 15 minutes. Serve warm.

Counter the creaminess of this tart with a high-toned wine with lively acidity, such as a young Italian wine from the Friuli region, like the delicious Sauvignon Blanc "Picol" 2001, which is produced by Lis Neris. Its citrusy aroma and mineral aftertaste will be just right.

Chicken Satay

with Spicy Peanut Sauce

Makes 4 servings

FOR THE SAUCE

2 Tbsp vegetable oil

2 shallots, finely chopped

1 clove garlic, finely chopped

1 small jalapeño chile, halved, seeded, and finely chopped

1 cup plus 3 Tbsp creamy peanut butter

½ cup unsweetened coconut milk

1 Tbsp Asian fish sauce (preferably nuoc nam)

2 Tbsp tamarind pulp or paste

2 tsp honey

FOR THE CHICKEN

1 Tbsp coriander seeds

2 tsp fennel seeds

1 stalk lemongrass, trimmed, outer leaves removed, and bulb thinly sliced

2 cloves garlic, finely chopped

2 Tbsp soy sauce

1 Tbsp Asian sesame oil

Freshly squeezed juice of ½ lime

2 tsp sugar

½ tsp turmeric

½ tsp salt

1 whole skinless, boneless chicken breast (about ¾ pound)

Sixteen 8-inch bamboo skewers, soaked in water for 30 minutes

The clean tropical-fruit flavors and midrange acidity of the 2001 Domaine du Clos Naudin, a Vouvray demi-sec, is soft on the palate while echoing the richness of the peanut sauce. Or the touch of sweetness offered by the German Riesling Selbach-Oster Spätlese Zeltinger Schlossberg 2001 also makes a good selection.

TO PREPARE THE SAUCE

Warm the vegetable oil in a small skillet over medium heat. Add the shallots, garlic, and chile and cook, stirring, until the shallots are tender and translucent, about 5 minutes. Reduce the heat to low and add the peanut butter, coconut milk, fish sauce, tamarind, and honey. Mix well; cook for 30 minutes, stirring occasionally. Transfer to a blender and puree until smooth. *(The sauce can be prepared up to 1 day ahead and stored in an airtight container in the refrigerator. Just before serving, rewarm the sauce.)*

TO PREPARE THE CHICKEN

Put the coriander and fennel seeds in a small skillet and cook over medium heat, periodically shaking the pan back and forth until toasted and fragrant, about 5 minutes. Finely grind in a spice grinder. Mix with the lemongrass, garlic, soy sauce, sesame oil, lime juice, sugar, turmeric, and salt.

Pour a third of the mixture into a shallow baking dish. Cut the chicken lengthwise into sixteen ¼-inch-thick strips and arrange them on top of the lemongrass mixture in a single layer in the dish. Pour the remaining marinade on top. Cover and refrigerate overnight.

Gently scrape the marinade off the chicken using the back of a knife. Thread a chicken slice onto each bamboo skewer. Heat a grill pan over medium-high heat until hot. Cook the chicken 1½ to 2 minutes on each side. Serve immediately with the peanut sauce.

Catalan Stuffed Tomatoes

Makes 6 servings

6 medium tomatoes
Salt
3 Tbsp extra-virgin olive oil
¼ cup chopped onion
½ pound ground pork or sausage
½ pound ground lamb
2 Tbsp fresh bread crumbs
1 Tbsp oil-packed sun-dried tomatoes,
    drained and finely chopped
1 clove garlic, finely chopped
½ sprig rosemary, leaves only, finely chopped
Pinch of hot pepper flakes
2½ to 3 cups unsalted chicken stock or
    low-sodium chicken broth
3 scallions, trimmed and cut into ½-inch pieces
⅓ cup diced (¼-inch cubes) red bell pepper
¼ cup diced (¼-inch cubes) zucchini
½ cup diced (¼-inch cubes) fennel bulb
¾ tsp loosely packed saffron threads
Freshly ground pepper
1 cup regular long-grain rice
1 sprig basil, leaves only

Center a rack in the oven and preheat to 375°F.

Slice about ¼ inch off the top of each tomato; set the tomato tops aside. Using a small spoon, scoop out the inside of each tomato and discard the seeds. Reserve any juice. Finely dice the tomato pulp and reserve for the stuffing. Sprinkle the inside of each tomato with ½ teaspoon salt and place upside down on a paper towel to drain.

Warm 1 teaspoon of olive oil in a small skillet over medium heat. Add the onion and cook, stirring, until tender and translucent, about 5 minutes.

Combine the diced tomatoes, onion, ground pork and lamb, bread crumbs, sun-dried tomatoes, garlic, rosemary, hot-pepper flakes, and 1 tablespoon of the olive oil in a bowl; season with salt. Stuff the tomatoes, forming a small mound on top. Place a reserved tomato top on each tomato and set aside.

Bring the chicken stock to a boil in a large saucepan over medium heat; reduce to a simmer.

Warm the remaining olive oil in a 13-by-9-inch roasting pan over medium heat. Add the scallions, red bell pepper, zucchini, fennel, and saffron, season with salt and pepper, and cook, stirring, for 4 to 5 minutes. Add the rice and continue to cook, stirring, for 2 to 3 minutes more. Pour the reserved tomato juices, and 2 cups of the simmering stock over the rice. Stir well and bring to a boil.

Place the stuffed tomatoes on top of the rice. Bake for 25 to 35 minutes, until the meat is golden brown and the rice is tender (add the remaining stock if the rice seems dry). Garnish with basil leaves just before serving.

VARIATION
For a more paella-like dish, add 1 pound scrubbed mussels or clams to the rice just before baking.

With this hearty summer preparation inspired by Catalunya, try a medium-bodied, low-acid (often a good choice with tomato dishes) Spanish wine like the Dominio de Atauta 2000 from the Ribera del Duero.

Melon Salad

with Lemongrass Shrimp

Makes 4 servings

1½ pounds large shrimp, peeled and deveined
6 Tbsp extra-virgin olive oil
2 tsp finely grated peeled ginger
2 tsp finely chopped lemongrass
Finely grated zest of 1 lime
Freshly squeezed juice of 2 limes
⅛ tsp Tabasco
Salt and freshly ground white pepper
1 ripe honeydew melon
1 ripe, small, round red watermelon
1 Tbsp finely chopped purple-basil leaves,
    plus additional small leaves
1 Tbsp finely chopped cilantro leaves,
    plus additional small leaves

The Chilean 1999 Santa Rita Reserva Sauvignon Blanc's high acidity, low alcohol content, and tropical-fruit scent add zing to the mellowness of the honeydew and cantaloupe. A more elegant choice would be the 1998 Kendall-Jackson Vintner's Reserve Chardonnay from Sonoma, California, whose rich toffee and butterscotch flavors retain a hint of fruitiness, keeping it lively on the palate.

Bring a pot of salted water to a boil, add shrimp, and cook for 3 to 5 minutes. Drain. When cool enough to handle, slice each shrimp in half lengthwise.

In a small bowl, whisk together the olive oil, ginger, lemongrass, lime zest and juice, and Tabasco. Season with salt and pepper. Set aside.

Halve the honeydew and watermelon, cut away the rind, and remove the seeds. Slice the melons into ⅛-inch-thick pieces. Remove the watermelon seeds (it's okay if the slices don't stay intact). Using a cake ring or a glass whose mouth is slightly smaller that than of a 14- to 16-ounce martini glass or champagne coupe, cut out 16 slices from the watermelon, and 16 slices from the honeydew. Save the best-looking 4 watermelon slices.

Set out four 8- to 12-ounce martini glasses or champagne coupes.

Layer two slices of watermelon and honeydew in each glass, lightly sprinkling each melon layer with the lemongrass dressing, chopped basil, chopped cilantro, salt, and pepper. (You may need to trim the melon slices so they fit neatly into the glasses, which should be half-full at this point.) Divide the shrimp among the glasses, arranging them in concentric circles. Season the shrimp with the dressing, basil, cilantro, salt, and pepper. Add another layer of melon in the reverse order: honeydew, then watermelon, seasoning as before. Top each salad with a reserved watermelon slice and sprinkle lightly with the dressing, basil, cilantro, salt, and pepper. Garnish with one basil and one cilantro leaf. Refrigerate for at least 1 hour before serving (the melon and shrimp taste best when well chilled).

COCKTAILS, SMALL BITES, AND STARTERS

Stuffed Artichokes

with Dungeness Crab and Chanterelles

Makes 4 servings

5 lemons: 4 halved, 1 peeled, segmented, and finely diced

4 large globe artichokes

Two 1½-pound Dungeness crabs or ¾ pound jumbo lump crabmeat

2 Tbsp extra-virgin olive oil

1 pound chanterelle mushrooms, trimmed and cleaned

3 shallots, minced

2 sprigs thyme, leaves only, chopped

3 Tbsp unsalted butter

4 sprigs tarragon, leaves only, three-fourths of the leaves chopped

Salt and freshly ground pepper

Pinch of cayenne

2 Tbsp minced chives

Bring a large pot of salted water to a boil; add the juice of 2 lemons.

Meanwhile, squeeze the juice of 1 lemon into a medium bowl and add 2 to 3 cups of water. Keep the bowl close at hand. Remove the tough outer leaves of one artichoke, leaving the tender inner leaves. Using a small sharp knife, trim the base of the artichoke until no dark-green areas remain. Trim the stem to 1 inch. Immediately drop the artichoke into the acidulated water to keep it from turning brown while you trim the other artichokes.

Drain the artichokes and lower them into the boiling water. Reduce the heat to a simmer and cook until the artichokes are tender when pierced with the tip of a knife, 25 to 30 minutes. Drain and set aside to cool.

Meanwhile, bring another large pot of salted water to a boil. Add the crabs and cook for 12 to 15 minutes. Drain and let cool. Pull off the top shells of one crab. Remove and discard the viscera, apron, and the feathery gills from the body. Rinse the crab thoroughly under cold running water. Break or cut the crab into two halves with the legs attached. Snap off the legs, leaving a portion of the body attached for easy handling. Crack the shell of the claws, legs, and the body, remove the meat and the tomalley; reserve the crab juices. Keep the leg meat separate from the rest of the crabmeat and discard the shells. Repeat with the remaining crabs. Push the tomalley through a fine-mesh sieve. Refrigerate the crabmeat, tomalley, and juices.

Warm 1 tablespoon of olive oil in a large skillet over high heat. Add the chanterelles, shallots, and thyme, and cook, stirring, until the mushrooms are tender and their juices have evaporated, 8 to 10 minutes. Remove from heat. Transfer half of the mushrooms to a food processor or blender. Add 2 tablespoons of the butter and the chopped tarragon, and season with salt and pepper. Puree until smooth. Set aside the puree and the remaining mushrooms.

Center a rack in the oven and preheat to 325°F. Brush a 13-by-9-inch baking dish with olive oil.

Cut each artichoke in half. Using a spoon, remove the chokes and the tiny center leaves. Mix together the chanterelle puree, crabmeat, tomalley, juice from the remaining lemon and the diced lemon. Fill each artichoke heart with the stuffing. Place the artichokes, stuffing-side up, in the baking dish and bake for 15 minutes. Combine the reserved chanterelles and leg meat and season with salt and pepper. Spoon the mixture around the artichokes and bake until the mushrooms and crab are heated through, about 5 minutes.

Bring the reserved crab juices, the remaining 1 tablespoon of olive oil, and the butter to a boil in a small saucepan. Season with the cayenne and stir in the chives.

To Serve

For each portion, place 2 artichoke halves on the center of a warm plate. Spoon the chanterelle-crab mixture over and around the stuffed artichokes. Drizzle on the reserved crab-juice sauce and sprinkle with the remaining tarragon leaves.

Artichokes can bring out a metallic taste in many wines, so a simple Rosé de Provence by Domaine Gavoty called "Cuvée Clarendon" is fruity, round and has a touch of earthiness that brings out the chanterelles.

Artichoke and Radicchio Clafoutis

Makes 6 servings

2 large eggs, at room temperature
3 large egg whites, at room temperature
4 tsp sugar
½ cup heavy cream
1 tsp firmly packed fresh yeast
¼ cup all-purpose flour
7 Tbsp extra-virgin olive oil
Freshly squeezed juice of 2 lemons
20 baby artichokes
2 ounces pancetta or bacon, diced into ¼-inch
  cubes (optional)
Salt and freshly ground pepper
8 white mushrooms, cleaned, trimmed, and cut
  into ¼-inch-thick slices
1 large shallot, finely chopped
2 ounces arugula, well washed, dried and trimmed
1 small head radicchio (about ¾ pound), trimmed
  and leaves separated

In a medium bowl, whisk together the eggs, egg whites, and sugar; set aside. Gently heat the heavy cream in a saucepan until barely warm. Remove from heat and add the yeast, stirring until smooth. Stir the cream into the egg mixture and whisk in the flour, followed by 2 tablespoons olive oil. Cover the batter with plastic wrap and refrigerate for 1 hour.

Combine the juice of 1 lemon and 2 cups water in a large bowl. Trim the artichoke stems, snap off the outer leaves until the remaining leaves are half yellow and half green. Cut off the remaining green parts and discard. Slice the artichokes lengthwise in half and drop into the lemon water.

Warm 1 tablespoon of olive oil in a medium skillet over high heat. When the pan is hot but not smoking, add the pancetta and cook, stirring frequently, for 1 minute. Drain the artichokes and add them to the pan along with the juice of half a lemon. Reduce the heat to medium and season with salt and pepper. Cover and cook, stirring occasionally, until the artichokes are tender, 10 to 12 minutes. Transfer to a plate.

Add 1 tablespoon olive oil to the pan. Add the mushrooms and shallot and season with salt and pepper. Cook for 3 minutes, tossing frequently. Add the arugula and one-quarter of the radicchio, season with salt and pepper, and cook, while tossing constantly, until the arugula and radicchio have wilted, about 2 minutes. Transfer the vegetables to a paper-towel-lined plate. When cool, coarsely chop the mushroom mixture.

Meanwhile, center a rack in the oven and preheat to 300°F.

Put a 6-by-2-inch round cake pan on a baking sheet. Spray the pan with nonstick cooking spray.

Stir the mushroom mixture into the clafoutis batter and season with salt and pepper. Pour half of the batter into the prepared pan and sprinkle the artichoke-pancetta mixture on top. Cover with the remaining batter (the pan should be about three-quarters full). Bake until a knife inserted in the middle comes out clean, 35 to 40 minutes.

Whisk together the remaining lemon juice and remaining 3 tablespoons olive oil. Toss the remaining radicchio with the lemon vinaigrette and season to taste with salt and pepper.

To Serve
Unmold the clafoutis, reinvert right side up, cut into 6 wedges, and serve hot, with the radicchio salad.

For this recipe, a round, creamy wine with melon aromas like the Loire Valley Vouvray Sec "Cuvée de Silex" from Domaine des Aubuisières 2001, is in order. Other Loire wines produced from Chenin Blanc grapes also go nicely with this type of dish.

Asparagus Four Ways
Steamed, Pan Roasted, Gratinéed, and Tempura

Each recipe makes 4 servings

FOR THE STEAMED ASPARAGUS
1 small bunch mint, leaves only
Salt
Zest of 1 lemon, removed with a vegetable peeler
16 pencil-thin stalks asparagus,
    peeled and trimmed
3 Tbsp extra-virgin olive oil
1 Tbsp freshly squeezed lemon juice
Freshly ground pepper

Bring about an inch of water to a boil in a large pot. Finely chop enough of the mint to equal ½ teaspoon; reserve. Salt the water and add the whole mint leaves and the lemon zest. Fit the pot with a steamer basket and add the asparagus. Cook until the asparagus is bright green and just tender, 2 to 3 minutes. Drain, discard the mint and lemon zest, and pat the asparagus dry.

Whisk together the olive oil, lemon juice, and chopped mint. Season to taste with salt and pepper and serve alongside the asparagus.

FOR THE ROASTED ASPARAGUS
4 slices prosciutto or ham
4 sticks of mozzarella, each about ¼-inch-thick,
    and ½-inch-wide and the same length as the
    asparagus
20 strips bacon
16 pencil-thin stalks asparagus, peeled,
    trimmed and steamed (see recipe above)
3 Tbsp extra-virgin olive oil

Put a slice of prosciutto on a work surface. Place 1 mozzarella stick at the long edge of the prosciutto and roll the meat around the cheese. Repeat with the rest of the prosciutto and cheese.

Line up 5 strips of bacon, long sides touching, on a work surface. Place two asparagus stalks crosswise on the bacon at one end, and one piece of prosciutto-wrapped cheese on the asparagus, then top with two more stalks of asparagus. Roll the bacon tightly around the bundle and tie in several places with kitchen twine. Repeat with the remaining bacon, prosciutto-wrapped cheese, and asparagus.

Warm the olive oil in a large skillet over medium heat. Cook the bundles, turning them frequently, until the bacon is golden and crisp, 4 to 5 minutes. Remove the string and serve immediately.

FOR THE GRATINÉED ASPARAGUS
1½ Tbsp unsalted butter
¼ cup finely chopped white or cremini
    mushrooms
1 cup fresh bread crumbs
¼ cup finely chopped, peeled and seeded
    tomatoes
1 Tbsp finely chopped flat-leaf parsley
1 Tbsp finely grated fresh Parmesan cheese
1 Tbsp finely chopped blanched almonds
Finely grated zest of 1 lemon
16 pencil-thin stalks asparagus, peeled, trimmed,
    and steamed (see recipe above left)

Melt the butter in a small skillet. Add the mushrooms and cook until tender, 4 to 5 minutes. Remove from heat and let cool for 20 minutes. Stir in the bread crumbs, tomato, parsley, Parmesan, almonds and lemon zest.

Preheat the broiler.

Arrange the asparagus in a single layer on a nonstick or foil-lined baking sheet. Sprinkle the breadcrumb mixture evenly over the asparagus and broil, until the crumb topping is golden, 2 to 3 minutes. Divide the gratinéed asparagus among warm dinner plates and serve immediately.

FOR THE ASPARAGUS TEMPURA

1 cup ice water
1 large egg yolk
⅔ cup cake flour (not self-rising)
⅔ cup rice flour
Peanut oil
16 pencil-thin stalks asparagus, peeled and
    trimmed

Whisk together the ice water and egg yolk in a medium bowl. Add the cake flour and rice flour, stirring lightly. Don't overmix—the batter should be very lumpy.

Pour 4 to 5 inches of oil into a deep pot and heat to 325°F as measured on a deep-fat thermometer. Line a baking sheet with a double thickness of paper towels.

Dip each asparagus spear into the batter and coat it with a thick lumpy layer. Lower the spears 4 at a time into the oil and cook until the batter is crisp but not colored, 3 to 4 minutes. Lift the asparagus out with a slotted spoon and drain on the paper towels. Repeat with the remaining asparagus. Serve hot.

The steamed and tempura asparagus call for an Alsatian wine like the 1998 Domaine Zind-Humbrecht Muscat Grand Cru Goldert, while the roasted and gratinéed spears—more robust dishes—will go well with a Tablas Creek Clos Blanc, Paso Robles 2000, an American white made with Marsanne, Roussanne, and Viognier grapes.

Waldorf Moderne

FOR THE APPLE GELÉE
4 Granny Smith apples, halved and cored

Pinch of vitamin-C powder (to keep the apples from turning brown; available in health-food stores)

½ tsp unflavored gelatin

FOR THE PINEAPPLE GELÉE
1 tsp unflavored gelatin

1 cup canned unsweetened pineapple juice

FOR THE SPICED PECANS
½ cup pecans

2 Tbsp light brown sugar

½ tsp ground cinnamon

Large pinch of cayenne

FOR THE DRESSING
¼ cup plus 1 Tbsp extra-virgin olive oil

¼ cup coarsely chopped onions

¼ cup peeled and coarsely chopped Gala apples

¼ cup coarsely chopped celery

¼ cup coarsely chopped fennel

2 tsp Madras curry powder

Pinch of saffron threads

Pinch of cayenne

¼ cup mayonnaise

¼ cup white-wine vinegar

Salt and freshly ground pepper

FOR THE SALAD
4 Belgian endives, trimmed and cut crosswise into 1-inch-thick slices

1 Gala apple, cored and diced into ½-inch cubes

3 stalks celery, peeled and cut diagonally into ¼-inch-thick slices

1 small fennel bulb, trimmed and thinly sliced

¼ cup candied-pineapple wedges (about ¼-inch-wide)

To Make the Apple Gelée

Cut one apple half into tiny cubes and set aside. Coarsely chop the remaining apples, put into a food processor, and puree until smooth. Add the vitamin-C powder and pulse to blend. Line a sieve with a double thickness of damp cheesecloth, set over a bowl, and pour in the puree. After the puree has strained, press against the solids with the back of a spoon to extract the last bit of juice. Discard the pulp and save the juice; you will need 1 cup.

Sprinkle the gelatin over 1 tablespoon cold water in a cup; let soften for 5 minutes. Warm the softened gelatin in the microwave oven on high for 15 seconds or until dissolved. Warm ¼ cup of the apple juice in the microwave. Stir in the gelatin, then stir in the remaining juice and the diced apple. Pour the gelée into a glass serving bowl and refrigerate until set, about 3 hours.

To Make the Pineapple Gelée

Sprinkle the gelatin over 1 tablespoon cold water in a cup; let soften for 5 minutes. Warm the softened gelatin in the microwave oven on high for 15 seconds or until dissolved. Warm ¼ cup of the pineapple juice in the microwave. Stir the gelatin into the warm juice, then stir in the remaining ¾ cup juice. Pour the gelée into a glass serving bowl and refrigerate until set, about 3 hours.

To Make the Spiced Pecans

Preheat the oven to 350°F. Toast the pecans on a baking sheet until golden brown, about 10 minutes.

Mix together the pecans, brown sugar, cinnamon, cayenne, and 1 teaspoon water in a small skillet over low heat. Cook, stirring, until the water evaporates and the nuts are nicely glazed. Transfer to a plate to cool.

To Make the Dressing

Warm 1 tablespoon of olive oil in a small skillet over medium heat. Add the onion, apple, celery, fennel, curry powder, saffron, and cayenne. Cook, stirring, until the vegetables are tender, 5 to 7 minutes. Let cool.

Put the apple-onion mixture, mayonnaise, vinegar, ¼ cup water and the remaining ¼ cup oil in a blender or food processor and puree until smooth (the dressing should lightly coat the back of a spoon). Season with salt and pepper; refrigerate until needed.

To Make the Salad

Toss together the ingredients in a large bowl.

To Serve

Place the bowls of dressing, gelée, pecans, and dressing around the salad, and let your guests assemble their own Waldorf Moderne.

The complexity of the salad's sweet, bitter, and spicy accents demand a wine that is crisp and fruity. My first instinct led me to whites from the Veneto region, specifically Gini La Frosca, a low-acid Soave Classico Superiore with a full, round flavor and a delightful citrus aroma. However, I am also partial to wines from New York's Finger Lakes region and recommend Hermann J. Wiemer's racy Johannisberg Riesling Dry. Still another option is from the famed apple-growing region of Normandy, France: Duché de Longueville cider, an inexpensive nonalcoholic alternative that deserves to be served in champagne flutes.

COCKTAILS, SMALL BITES, AND STARTERS

Spiced Beef Borscht

Makes 6 servings

2 tsp each fennel, coriander, cumin, and caraway
  seeds

¾ cup crème fraîche

2 Tbsp unsalted butter

1 medium onion, diced into ½-inch cubes

2 medium leeks, white and light-green parts
  only, trimmed, washed, dried, and diced
  into ½-inch cubes

2 large stalks celery, peeled and diced into
  ½-inch cubes

½ small fennel bulb, trimmed and diced into
  ½-inch cubes

¼ small head green cabbage, cored and diced
  into ½-inch cubes

3 large beets, peeled, trimmed and diced into
  ½-inch cubes

10 cups unsalted chicken stock or low-sodium
  chicken broth

Salt and freshly ground pepper

8 ounces lean sirloin, diced into ½-inch cubes

2 Tbsp extra-virgin olive oil

4 slices firm-textured white bread, crusts
  removed, diced into ¼-inch cubes (about
  1 cup)

Put 1½ teaspoons each of the seeds (fennel, coriander, cumin, and caraway) onto a square of cheesecloth and tie with kitchen string to make a spice sachet. Combine and grind the remaining ½ teaspoon each of the seeds in a spice grinder, fold into the crème fraîche, and refrigerate.

Melt the butter in a large pot over medium heat. Add the onion, leeks, celery, and fennel; cook, stirring, until the vegetables soften, 5 to 7 minutes. Add the cabbage, beets, spice sachet, and chicken stock. Bring to a boil and season with salt and pepper. Reduce the heat and simmer until the beets are tender, about 35 minutes. Remove the sachet and add the beef. Cook 5 minutes more.

Meanwhile, warm the olive oil in a small nonstick skillet over medium heat. Toss in the bread and season with salt and pepper. Cook, stirring, until the bread is crisp and golden brown. Drain the croutons on paper towels.

To Serve
Ladle the borscht into warm soup bowls and top with a spoonful of the spiced crème fraîche and a scattering of croutons.

Napa Valley Zinfandels, like those from Storybook Mountain Vineyards, are known for their deep color, good fruit, and spice, all of which make them a great choice for the Spiced Beef Borscht.

Spring Root–Vegetable Potage
with Sorrel

Makes 4 servings

2 Tbsp unsalted butter

2 cups peeled and thinly sliced spring onions
(about 4)

Salt and freshly ground white pepper

3 cups new potatoes (1 to 1½ pounds), peeled
and diced into ½-inch cubes

1 cup turnips (about ½ pound), peeled, trimmed,
and diced into ½-inch cubes

1 cup radishes (about 12), trimmed and diced
into ½-inch cubes

6 to 7 cups unsalted chicken stock or low-sodium
chicken broth

Melt the butter in a large pot over medium heat.
Add the onions, season with salt and pepper, and
cook until translucent, 10 to 12 minutes. Add the
potatoes, turnips, and radishes, and season again.
Cook, stirring, 5 to 6 minutes more. Add the
chicken stock and bring to a boil. Reduce the heat
and simmer until the vegetables are very tender
and falling apart, about 45 minutes.

Puree the liquid and vegetables in batches in a
blender until smooth. If the soup is too thick, add
an additional ½ to 1 cup of stock. Taste and season
with salt and pepper if needed.

To Serve

4 ounces sorrel, leaves only, julienned

4 Tbsp crème fraîche

1 egg yolk

Salt and freshly ground white pepper

In a blender, puree 2 ounces of the sorrel, crème
fraîche, and yolk until smooth and season with salt
and pepper. Ladle the potage into warm soup
bowls, sprinkle liberally with the remaining sorrel,
and drizzle with the sorrel-crème fraîche mixture.

*The mellow flavors of the potage will benefit from
the mineral element and discreet melon aromas of a
Loire Valley Vouvray Sec, such as a 2001 vintage from
Domaine Foreau.*

Saffron-Infused Mussel Velouté
with Mussels Gratins

Makes 4 servings

1 Tbsp unsalted butter

3 shallots, thinly sliced

2 pounds mussels, scrubbed

1½ cups dry white wine

Freshly ground pepper

FOR THE MUSSEL VELOUTÉ

2 Tbsp unsalted butter

2 Tbsp extra-virgin olive oil

2 medium onions, thinly sliced

1 large fennel bulb, trimmed and thinly sliced

2 stalks celery, peeled, trimmed, and thinly sliced

1 medium leek, white and light-green parts only, thinly sliced, rinsed, and dried

1 large carrot, thinly sliced

1 large Idaho potato, peeled and cut into small pieces

1 cup heavy cream

Large pinch of saffron threads

Sachet (1 tsp each fennel seeds, coriander seeds, and white peppercorns, 1 bay leaf, 2 sprigs thyme, and 4 sprigs flat-leaf parsley, tied in cheesecloth)

4 cups unsalted chicken stock or low-sodium chicken broth

Salt and freshly ground white pepper

FOR THE CRUST

¾ cup fresh bread crumbs

1 stick plus 2 Tbsp unsalted butter, at room temperature

2 Tbsp finely chopped flat-leaf parsley

4 cloves garlic, finely chopped

1 Tbsp finely chopped toasted almonds

1 Tbsp finely chopped speck ham or prosciutto

Salt and freshly ground white pepper

Melt the butter in a Dutch oven or large pot over medium heat. Add the shallots and cook, stirring, until translucent, about 5 minutes. Increase the heat to high and add the mussels and white wine. Season with pepper. Cover and cook, stirring a few times, until the mussels open, 3 to 4 minutes.

Meanwhile, place a cheesecloth-lined sieve over a large bowl. When all the mussels have opened, turn the mussels and liquid into the sieve. Reserve the mussels and broth separately. When the mussels are cool enough to handle, remove the meat from the shells. Discard the shells and cover the mussels (refrigerate them if you are not making the soup right away).

TO MAKE THE MUSSEL VELOUTÉ

Melt the butter with the oil in a large pot over medium-high heat. Add the onions and cook, stirring, until translucent, 5 to 7 minutes. Add the fennel, celery, leek, carrot, and potato, and cook until tender, 15 to 20 minutes. Add the heavy cream, saffron, sachet, reserved mussel liquid, and chicken stock, and season with salt and pepper; bring to a boil. Reduce to a simmer and cook, skimming regularly, until all the vegetables are tender, about 20 minutes.

Working in batches, puree the soup in a blender. Push the puree through a fine-mesh sieve set over a bowl, then season with salt and pepper. *(The soup can be refrigerated for 4 days or frozen for a month.)* Bring to a boil before serving.

TO MAKE THE CRUST AND GRATINS

Mix together the bread crumbs, butter, parsley, garlic, almonds, and ham in a bowl until blended. Season with salt and pepper. Roll out the mixture between two pieces of parchment paper to form a 4-inch square about ¼ inch thick. Transfer the packet to a small baking sheet and freeze for at

least 30 minutes, then cut the crust into four squares; refrigerate until needed.

Preheat the broiler, and butter a large gratin dish. Put a 2-inch cake ring or biscuit cutter in the gratin dish and fill with a quarter of the mussels. Lift out the ring and top the mussels with a square of crust. Repeat to make 3 more mussels gratins. Broil the gratins, watching them closely, until the tops are golden brown, 2 to 4 minutes.

To Serve
Bring the velouté to a boil. Transfer each gratin to the center of a warm soup bowl. Ladle the hot soup around the mussels and serve immediately.

Mas Daumas-Gassac in the Languedoc produces a full-bodied white wine based on Roussanne and Marsanne grapes with floral aromas that hold up well against the saffron and cream in the velouté.

COCKTAILS, SMALL BITES, AND STARTERS

Penne with Morels
and Spring Peas, Bacon, and Eggs

Makes 4 servings

1 pound penne pasta
5 ounces snow peas, trimmed (about 1 cup)
5 ounces fresh English peas, shelled (about 1 cup)
3 Tbsp unsalted butter
3 medium shallots, peeled and finely chopped
1½ cups unsalted chicken stock or low-sodium
   chicken broth
1 cup heavy cream
Salt and freshly ground pepper
1 pound morel (or white) mushrooms, washed
   thoroughly and trimmed
4 strips smoked bacon
5 large eggs in the shell
2 Tbsp unsalted butter

Bring a large pot of salted water to a boil. Cook the pasta until almost al dente. Drain; keep warm.

Fill the same pot with salted water and bring to a boil. Add the snow peas and English peas and cook for 5 minutes. Drain the peas in a colander and run cold water over them until cool; drain.

Melt 1 tablespoon of the butter in a large skillet over medium heat. Add one-third of the shallots and cook until translucent, about 2 minutes. Add half of the English and snow peas, 1 cup of the stock, and the cream, and season with salt and pepper. Cook until the peas are very soft, 7 to 10 minutes. Transfer the mixture to a blender and puree until smooth. Taste and season with salt and pepper if needed. Set aside.

Wipe the inside of the skillet clean. Melt the remaining 2 tablespoons butter over medium-low heat. Add the remaining shallots and cook until translucent, about 2 minutes. Add the morels and cook, while stirring, until very tender, about 10 minutes. Season with salt and pepper and transfer to a bowl.

Again, wipe the inside of the skillet clean and warm over medium-high heat. Add the bacon and cook on both sides until crisp, 3 to 4 minutes. Drain on paper towels. *(The bacon can be served whole or finely chopped.)*

Bring a medium pot of water to a boil. Gently slip in the eggs and cook for 4 minutes until soft-boiled. Remove four eggs from the pot and run under cold water to cool. Boil the remaining egg for another 6 minutes. Remove it from the pot and run under cold water to cool. Gently peel all the eggs. Leave the soft-cooked eggs whole and finely chop the hard-cooked egg.

Combine the butter, pasta, morels, the rest of the peas, and the remaining ½ cup stock in a large skillet. Cook, tossing, over medium heat for a few minutes until heated through. Taste and season with salt and pepper. Rewarm the pea cream in a saucepan while whisking continuously

To Serve
Divide the pasta mixture among four warm shallow bowls and spoon the pea cream over it. Place a soft-cooked egg in the center of the dish and serve the chopped egg and bacon alongside.

A young wine with good acidity will emphasize the freshness of the spring peas and have enough richness to stand up to the egg and cream. Two nutty white burgundies from Domaine Caillot in the village of Mersault will complement the dish beautifully: La Barre Dessus Clos Marguerite 2000, which carries the highly regarded Mersault appellation, and the more affordable Les Herbeux 2000.

Asparagus and Shrimp Risotto

Makes 4 servings

16 spears asparagus, peeled and trimmed
6 cups unsalted chicken stock or low-sodium chicken broth
1 Tbsp extra-virgin olive oil
1 clove garlic, crushed
1 sprig rosemary
16 small Gulf shrimp, peeled, deveined, and each cut into 3 pieces
Salt and freshly ground pepper
4 Tbsp unsalted butter
¼ cup finely chopped white onion
1 cup Arborio rice
½ cup dry vermouth or dry white wine
2 Tbsp finely grated fresh Parmesan cheese
2 Tbsp mascarpone cheese

Cut off the top 2 inches of each asparagus spear and set aside. Cut the next 2 to 3 inches of each spear into ¼-inch-thick pieces; discard the remaining portion.

Meanwhile, bring a large pot of salted water to a boil. Add the asparagus rounds and blanch for 4 minutes. Drain, and run under cold water until cool, then set aside.

Put 4 asparagus tips, a quarter of the asparagus rounds, and 3 tablespoons of water in a blender and purée until smooth. Set aside.

Pour the chicken stock into a large saucepan and bring to a boil over medium heat; reduce the heat to a simmer.

The medium-bodied 1996 Savennières-Becherelle from Domaine du Clos de la Coulée de Serrant is unrivalled as a companion to the risotto, but other Loire Valley wines produced from Chenin Blanc could also be served.

Warm the olive oil in a medium skillet over medium heat. Add the remaining asparagus tips, garlic, and rosemary, and cook, tossing, until the asparagus is tender but still crisp, about 3 minutes. Add the shrimp and continue to cook until cooked through, 3 to 5 minutes; season with salt and pepper. Discard the garlic and rosemary; set aside and keep warm.

Melt 2 tablespoons of the butter in a large saucepan over medium-low heat. Add the onion and cook, stirring with a wooden spoon, until the onion is translucent, about 5 minutes. Add the rice and cook, stirring, for about 5 minutes longer. Add the vermouth, and stir, scraping the bottom of the pot. Cook, stirring once or twice, until the liquid has evaporated. Add 1 cup of the simmering stock. Cook, stirring often, until the rice absorbs most of the liquid. Add another cup of the hot stock. Continue cooking, stirring, and adding the stock, 1 cup at a time, until 5 cups have been added. At this point, taste the rice. Usually, the rice will need another ½ to 1 cup stock and a few more minutes to cook.

Stir in the remaining 2 tablespoons of butter, the Parmesan, mascarpone, and the asparagus puree. Add the remaining asparagus rounds and stir to warm the asparagus; remove from heat. Season with salt and pepper if needed. Cover and keep warm.

Warm the olive oil in a medium skillet over medium heat. Add the remaining asparagus tips, garlic, and rosemary and cook, while tossing, until the asparagus is tender but still crisp, about 3 minutes. Add the shrimp and continue to cook until cooked through, 3 to 5 minutes; season with salt and pepper. Discard the garlic and rosemary.

To Serve
Spoon the risotto into warm soup plates and top with the warmed asparagus tips and shrimp. Serve immediately.

Fish and Shellfish

At DANIEL we're able to serve an incredible array of fish and shellfish because we have established long-term relationships with several trusted suppliers—variety counts for little without freshness. But you don't have to run a restaurant to get the best fish, just get to know your local fishmonger. The success of the seafood dishes you prepare will depend on it.

Since fish cooks quickly and its flesh is easily flavored, it requires a delicate touch, but the same qualities also make it an exceptionally versatile food. A humble cod fillet, for example, lends itself beautifully to simple searing in olive oil with garlic and black pepper. With a little more effort, however, and a few additional ingredients—sweet onions, Dijon mustard, or mushrooms, to name a few—you can have Cod Lyonnaise, Dijonnaise, or Bordelaise. Similarly, clementines give my Caramelized Bay Scallops a citrusy lift, while mussels bring a briny flavor to the Stuffed Skate.

While fish is often considered a special-occasion dish, it doesn't have to be confined to the dinner table. The fennel- and radish-seasoned Lobster Rolls are perfect for an outing in the park, and my Vietnamese Crab Spring Rolls, flavored with mango, Serrano chilis, and lime juice, deliver a spicy Asian zing that would make a lovely treat while waiting for a tuna steak to come off the grill.

Finally, every home chef should try preparing a whole fish on the bone. The cooking process is gentle, the flesh remains moist, and few things are as satisfying. Unwrapping the bamboo leaves from my whole Red Snapper and releasing that first puff of lemongrass-, cilantro-, and mint-infused steam will no doubt impress your guests, not to mention fill you with an unforgettable sense of accomplishment.

Caramelized Bay Scallops
with Clementines and Cauliflower

Makes 4 servings

1 head cauliflower (about 1 pound), trimmed, cut into 1-inch florets, stems peeled, and cut into ½-inch-thick slices

Salt and freshly ground pepper

8 Tbsp (1 stick) unsalted butter

2 Tbsp extra-virgin olive oil

2 dozen bay scallops (about 2 pounds)

Freshly squeezed juice of 1 lemon

4 clementines, peeled and segmented

Julienned zest of 4 kumquats

3 Tbsp Sicilian capers, soaked in cold water for 20 minutes, rinsed and drained

1 Tbsp finely chopped flat-leaf parsley

Bring a medium saucepan of salted water to a boil. Add the cauliflower and cook until tender, 7 to 9 minutes. Drain well.

Put the cauliflower into a food processor and puree until smooth, taking care not to overwork the mixture. Season with salt and pepper and stir in 4 tablespoons of the butter. Transfer the puree to the top of a double boiler, press a piece of plastic wrap against the surface of the puree and set aside.

Warm the remaining 4 tablespoons butter and the olive oil in a large skillet over high heat. Pat the scallops dry, season with salt and pepper, and slip them into the pan. Cook, turning the scallops as necessary, until they are golden on all sides and just cooked through, 4 to 5 minutes. Deglaze the pan with the lemon juice. Add the clementines, kumquat zest, capers, and parsley to the pan. Season with salt and pepper and cook, stirring, until heated through, about 1 minute.

To Serve
Divide the cauliflower puree among four warm soup plates. Arrange the bay scallops on top and spoon on the clementine-kumquat mixture. Serve immediately.

Scallops tend to work well with richer Chardonnays and the tropical-fruit flavors in the Hanzell from Sonoma, California, which also combines nicely with the clementines and kumquats. The capers add a nice touch of acidity at the end that enlivens the wine.

Soft Shell Crabs

with Sorrel Cream

Makes 4 servings

⅓ cup heavy cream, whipped

8 ounces sorrel, stems and center veins removed, washed, dried, and cut into ½-inch-wide strips

Salt and freshly ground white pepper

3 Tbsp unsalted butter

4 medium spring onions, white and light-green parts only, thinly sliced

2 cloves garlic, crushed

6 ounces spinach, stems and center veins removed, washed, dried, and cut into ½-inch-wide strips

6 ounces arugula, stems and center veins removed, washed, dried, and cut into ½-inch-wide strips

6 ounces romaine lettuce, stems and center veins removed, washed, dried, and cut into ½-inch-wide strips

8 live medium soft-shell crabs (ask your fishmonger to remove the gills, tails, eyes, and soft innards)

1 Tbsp extra-virgin olive oil

All-purpose flour for dredging

2 plum tomatoes, peeled, seeded, and diced into ¼-inch cubes

The sorrel's acidity requires a wine that complements and even mellows it. The 2001 Pouilly-Fumé Vieilles Vignes Domaine Caillebourdin, with its smoky bouquet, makes a suitable choice.

Whisk the heavy cream in a mixing bowl until soft peaks form. Put one-third of the sorrel into a blender and puree until smooth, adding 1 or 2 tablespoons of water if necessary. Gently fold the sorrel puree into the whipped cream, season with salt and pepper, and refrigerate.

Warm 2 tablespoons of the butter in a large skillet over medium-low heat. Add the onions and garlic, and season with salt and pepper. Cook, stirring, until the onion softens but is not brown, 5 to 7 minutes. Add the spinach, increase the heat to high, and toss until the spinach just starts to wilt, 1 to 2 minutes. Add the arugula, cook for 1 minute more, still stirring and tossing; add the romaine. Cook for another 2 minutes, drain off any excess liquid from the pan, then add the remaining sorrel and more salt and pepper if needed. Cook until the sorrel wilts and everything is tender, 1 to 2 minutes. Remove from heat, discard the garlic, and set the greens aside, keeping them warm.

Rinse the crabs well and pat dry. Warm the olive oil in a large skillet over high heat. Season the crabs with salt and pepper and dredge in the flour, shaking off any excess. Put them in the pan and cook until lightly browned, about 3 minutes. Add the remaining tablespoon butter and flip the crabs over, cooking for 2 minutes more. Add the tomatoes and cook for another minute.

To Serve

Divide the greens among four warm dinner plates and top each mound with 2 soft-shell crabs and some diced tomato. Spoon the sorrel cream on top and serve immediately.

Stuffed Skate

with Mussels, Potatoes, and Saffron Butter

Makes 4 servings

7 Tbsp unsalted butter, at room temperature
2 pinches of saffron threads
Salt and freshly ground pepper
3 Tbsp extra-virgin olive oil
10 white mushrooms, trimmed and thinly sliced
1 small onion or 2 small shallots, peeled
2 bunches arugula (about 5 to 6 ounces each), leaves only
8 to 12 fingerling potatoes (about 10 ounces)
Four 8-ounce skate wing fillets, boned and skinned
1 pound mussels (about 32), scrubbed
¼ cup slivered almonds
Finely chopped flat-leaf parsley leaves for garnish

Saffron's assertiveness, when allied with the slight bitterness of arugula, calls for a dry wine with mineral overtones and citrus aromas. Dry Bordeaux, such as a Château Carbonnieux from the Graves area, tend to have broad flavors and good body despite their acidity, making them tempting candidates for this complex and flavorful dish.

Melt 2 tablespoons of the butter with 2 teaspoons of water in a small saucepan. Add the saffron, remove from the heat, and infuse until the butter turns red. Strain the butter through a fine-mesh sieve, discard the saffron, and let the butter cool. Mix the infused butter with the remaining 5 tablespoons butter. Season with salt and pepper. Roll the butter mixture out between two pieces of parchment paper or plastic wrap into a 6-inch square. Refrigerate until firm.

Warm the olive oil in a large skillet over medium heat. Add the mushrooms and cook, stirring, for 4 minutes. Add the onion and cook 2 minutes more. Add the arugula leaves and cook just until wilted, 3 to 5 minutes. Season with salt and pepper. Remove from heat. When cool, finely chop the vegetables.

Meanwhile, put the potatoes into a large pot with enough salted water to cover them and bring to a boil. Cook until they are tender, 15 to 20 minutes. Drain and keep warm.

Center a rack in the oven and preheat to 375°F. Butter a 13-by-9-inch baking pan.

Season the underside of the skate wings (the red part). Put an equal portion of the vegetable mixture in the center of each fillet, fold in half, and season with salt and pepper. Cut the saffron butter into 8 equal pieces. Place 2 pieces in the bottom of the prepared pan. Put the fillets in the pan and distribute the remaining butter evenly over the fish. Scatter the mussels, potatoes, and almonds around the fish. Bake for 12 to 15 minutes until the mussels open and the fish is just cooked through. Remove from the oven, sprinkle with the parsley, and serve immediately.

Cod

Lyonnaise, Dijonnaise, and Bordelaise

Makes 4 servings

FOR THE SEARED COD
1 Tbsp extra-virgin olive oil
Four 6-ounce center-cut cod fillets, skin left on
Salt and freshly ground pepper
4 cloves garlic, lightly crushed
4 sprigs thyme
1 Tbsp unsalted butter

Warm the olive oil in a large nonstick skillet over medium-high heat. Season the fillets with salt and pepper and slip them into the pan, skin side down, along with the garlic and thyme. Sear the fillets for 3 minutes, turn them over and cook for 3 minutes more. Reduce the heat to medium, add the butter and cook another 3 minutes, or until the fish is opaque, moist, and lightly firm when pressed. Serve immediately.

FOR THE COD LYONNAISE
3 Tbsp extra-virgin olive oil
1½ pounds Yukon Gold potatoes, peeled, and diced into ½-inch cubes
1½ pounds sweet onions, diced into ½-inch cubes
Salt and freshly ground pepper
2 Tbsp red-wine vinegar
1 recipe Seared Cod
6 sprigs flat-leaf parsley, leaves finely chopped

Warm the olive oil in a large nonstick skillet over medium-high heat. Add the potatoes and cook, tossing, for 10 minutes. Add the onions, season with salt and pepper, and cook until the onions are translucent and the potatoes are tender, 5 to 10 minutes. Pour in the vinegar and cook until it has reduced to a glaze. Spoon onto a serving platter, top with the seared cod, and sprinkle with the parsley.

FOR THE COD DIJONNAISE
1½ pounds carrots, peeled and thinly sliced
1½ pounds spinach, washed and stemmed
1 Tbsp unsalted butter
Salt and freshly ground white pepper
1 recipe Seared Cod
2 Tbsp Dijon mustard
1 cup fresh bread crumbs
2 Tbsp minced chives
1 Tbsp extra-virgin olive oil

Bring a large pot of salted water to a boil. Add the carrots and cook for 5 minutes. Add the spinach and cook for 1 minute more; drain well and squeeze the excess water from the spinach. Melt the butter in a large skillet over medium heat. Add the carrots and spinach and season with salt and pepper. Cook until well coated with the butter. Spoon onto a serving platter and keep warm.

Preheat the broiler. Place the seared cod in a foil-lined broiler pan. Spread the mustard evenly over the fillets. Mix together the bread crumbs, chives, and olive oil and pat evenly over the fish. Broil just until the crumbs are golden brown. Place the cod on top of the vegetables and serve immediately.

FOR THE COD BORDELAISE
1 recipe Seared Cod
2 Tbsp unsalted butter
½ cup finely chopped shallots
12 ounces sliced seasonal mushrooms
2 sprigs thyme
½ bottle dry red wine

For the Bordelaise, a medium-bodied Haut-Médoc such as the 1994 Château Sociando-Mallet; for the Dijonnaise, a Mâcon-Clessé Quintaine Cuvée 1998 from Jean Thevenet; and for the Lyonnaise, the 2000 Sauvignon de Saint-Bris from Goisot.

Warm the butter in a large skillet over medium-high heat. Add the shallots and cook until translucent, about 5 minutes. Add the mushrooms and thyme and cook 5 minutes longer. Add the wine and cook until the liquid is reduced by half. Discard the thyme. Transfer the cod to a warm platter and spoon the mushroom mixture on top. Serve immediately.

Spicy Sea Bass

with Olive-Crushed Potatoes

Makes 4 servings

1 pound Yukon Gold potatoes

3 Tbsp unsalted butter

3 Tbsp extra-virgin olive oil

¼ cup quartered, pitted Niçoise olives

¼ cup coarsely chopped flat-leaf parsley leaves

Finely grated zest and juice of 1 lemon

4 tsp capers, drained

½ tsp piment d'Espelette or ¼ tsp sweet paprika
  and ¼ tsp cayenne

Salt and freshly ground pepper

Four 6-ounce sea bass, flounder, grouper, or
  snapper fillets

1 Tbsp minced chives or scallions

1 lemon, cut in wedges

Center a rack in the oven and preheat to 325°F.

Place the potatoes on a baking sheet and bake until very tender, 40 to 50 minutes. Peel while still warm and transfer to a bowl. Using a fork, coarsely crush the potatoes with 2 tablespoons of the butter, 2 tablespoons of olive oil, and half each of the olives, parsley, lemon zest and juice, capers, and piment d'Espelette. Season with salt and pepper and transfer to a large serving platter. Set aside and keep warm.

Warm the remaining tablespoon of olive oil in a large nonstick skillet over medium heat. Season the fish fillets with salt and pepper and slip them into the pan, skin side down. Cook for 2 to 3 minutes. Turn the fillets over, add the remaining tablespoon of butter, and continue to cook for 2 to 3 minutes (if the fillets are very thick, cover the pan with a lid while cooking the second side). Arrange the fillets on top of the potatoes and keep warm. Toss the remaining olives, parsley, lemon zest and juice, capers, piment d'Espelette, and chives with the pan juices, and season with salt and pepper.

To Serve

Spoon the olive mixture over the fish, garnish with the lemon wedges, and serve immediately.

A medium-bodied California Sauvignon Blanc, which tends to be creamy yet zesty, seems a perfect choice. Westerly Vineyards in the Santa Ynez Valley, for instance, will stand up to this intricate dish without stealing the show.

Eggplant–Wrapped Swordfish
with Tomato and Meyer Lemon

Makes 4 servings

½ pint cherry tomatoes
2 Japanese or Italian eggplants
One 1-pound swordfish steak, cut into 8 even
    rectangles (3 to 4 inches long and 1 inch wide)
Salt and freshly ground pepper
5 sprigs fresh basil; half leaves chopped,
    half leaves kept whole
1 Meyer or regular lemon
4 Tbsp extra-virgin olive oil
1 small red bell pepper, finely diced
1 small yellow bell pepper, finely diced
1 small green bell pepper, finely diced
2 small zucchini, finely diced

Bring a saucepan of water to a boil. Cut a small X in the base of each tomato and add them to the boiling water. Blanch for 5 to 10 seconds. Drain the tomatoes and run under cold water to cool. Using a small knife, peel the tomatoes.

Using a mandoline, cut each eggplant lengthwise into very thin slices. Place 5 eggplant slices on a work surface so that their long sides overlap slightly. Season the swordfish with salt and pepper. Lay one swordfish rectangle crosswise at the end of the eggplant. Sprinkle the fish with some chopped basil. Carefully roll up the fish, very tightly, in the eggplant. Trim the edges evenly and place the fish on a plate, seam side down. Repeat with the remaining swordfish, eggplant, and basil.

Remove the zest from the lemon using a vegetable peeler and cut into very thin strips. Working over a small bowl, segment the lemon. Set aside. Bring a small pot of water to a boil. Add the zest and blanch for 4 to 5 minutes. Drain and repeat one more time. Drain the zest and set aside.

Warm 1 tablespoon of the olive oil in a medium skillet over medium heat. Add the bell peppers and cook, without color, for 4 to 5 minutes. Add the zucchini and cook until the vegetables are tender, 3 to 4 minutes. Season with salt and pepper. Transfer the vegetables to a bowl and keep warm.

Wipe clean the inside of the skillet. Warm 1 tablespoon of olive oil over medium-high heat. When the oil is hot, place the wrapped swordfish in the pan, seam side down. As it cooks, drizzle oil over the swordfish; add more as it is absorbed, about 1½ tablespoons should be enough. When golden on each side, the fish should be cooked to perfection. Remove and keep warm. Add the remaining ½ tablespoon oil to the pan and toss in the cherry tomatoes and the rest of the chopped basil. Season with salt and pepper if needed.

To Serve
Put the peppers and zucchini on the bottom of a warm serving dish. Place the swordfish on top and sprinkle with the lemon zest and segment. Add the cherry tomatoes, and garnish with the whole basil leaves.

A full-bodied Chardonnay will hold up superbly to the swordfish. Domaine la Bongran in Burgundy makes a great Mâcon-Villages with a lot of extract and well-rounded buttery flavors that give more dimension to the fish. The Meyer lemon in the preparation adds the final kick.

Vietnamese Crab Spring Rolls

Makes about 24 spring rolls

1 large ripe mango, peeled, pitted, and chopped
½ Serrano chile pepper, finely grated
Freshly squeezed juice of ½ lime
Salt
8 ounces Peekytoe, Dungeness, or Blue crabmeat,
    picked over to remove shell
¼ cup mayonnaise
Finely grated zest of 1 lime
Freshly ground pepper
½ cup 3-inch-long jicama julienne
½ cup 3-inch-long red bell pepper julienne
½ cup 3-inch-long carrot julienne
½ cup 3-inch-long celery julienne
½ cup 3-inch-long seedless-cucumber julienne
2 Tbsp chopped mint leaves
2 Tbsp chopped cilantro leaves
2 Tbsp chopped chives
Twenty-four 6-inch-round rice-paper wrappers
3 Tbsp chopped toasted, salted peanuts

Put the mango, Serrano chile pepper, and lime juice in a blender and puree until smooth; season with salt. Transfer to a covered container and refrigerate. *(The sauce can be made ahead and stored in an airtight container in the refrigerator for up to 2 days.)*

Combine the crab, mayonnaise, and lime zest in a bowl; season with salt and pepper. In another bowl, mix together the jicama, red bell pepper, carrot, celery, cucumber, mint, cilantro, and chives; season with salt and pepper.

To Make the Spring Rolls
Soak 1 or 2 rice-paper wrappers in a large bowl of hot water, just until pliable, about 15 minutes. Drain and place the softened wrappers on a dry kitchen towel with the rounded edges toward you. Place 2 tablespoons of the vegetables 1 inch from the bottom edge. Top with 1 tablespoon of the seasoned crab, sprinkle with peanuts, and season with pepper. Fold the bottom edge over the filling and roll up tightly. Cover the finished rolls with a damp kitchen towel. Repeat, soaking and filling the remaining wrappers and changing the water as necessary.

To Serve
Trim off the ends of the crab rolls and cut each in half on the bias. Serve with the mango sauce.

Simple flavors and freshness are the hallmarks of this dish, and a medium bodied, floral Pinot Gris from Alsace with its touch of sweetness seems the right match. Those made by Domaine Paul Blanck have all these attributes as well as a good core of acidity and some tropical-fruit aromas that blend nicely with the mango sauce.

Clam, Tuna, and Potato Marinière

Makes 4 servings

1 bunch flat-leaf parsley, leaves only
3 Tbsp extra-virgin olive oil
1 shallot, finely chopped
24 littleneck clams, scrubbed
1 cup dry white wine
Freshly ground pepper
1 pound spring potatoes, peeled, diced into
    ¼-inch cubes, and kept in water
2 Tbsp unsalted butter
Salt
One 8-ounce tuna-loin steak, skinned,
    and cut into 8 slices

Prepare an ice-water bath in a medium bowl. Bring a medium pot of water to a boil. Add the parsley and cook until tender, about 5 minutes. Drain and add the parsley to the ice-water bath. Drain again. Transfer the parsley to a food processor or blender, add 2 tablespoons water, and puree until smooth. Set aside.

Warm 2 tablespoons olive oil in a large Dutch oven or pot over medium heat. Add the shallot and cook, stirring, for 2 minutes. Add the clams and wine and season with pepper. Cover and bring to a boil. Cook for 5 to 10 minutes, transferring the clams to a bowl as they open. Discard any clams that don't open. When cool enough to handle, remove the clam meat. Separately set aside the clam meat, clam broth, and 4 large shell halves. Discard the remaining shells.

Meanwhile, bring the potatoes to a boil in a large pot of salted water. Cook until tender, 15 to 20 minutes. Drain.

Add the reserved clam broth to the same pot, reduce the liquid by half over high heat. Stir in the butter and parsley puree and season with salt and pepper. Add the reserved clam meat and potatoes and cook until heated through. Season with salt and pepper if needed.

Warm the remaining tablespoon of olive oil in a small skillet over medium-high heat. Season the tuna slices with salt and pepper. Slip into the pan and cook for 15 seconds; flip and cook for another 15 seconds.

To Serve
Divide the clams and potatoes among four warm soup bowls. Place 2 tuna slices in each bowl and spoon in the warm clam broth. Serve immediately.

This seafood combination requires a lighter white Burgundy such as the Bourgogne-Chardonnay "Les Herbeux" from Domaine Caillot, whose restrained buttery aromatic profile and mineral overtones hold their own with the tuna but don't overwhelm the broth and clams.

Seafood à l'Orientale

Makes 4 servings

FOR THE BEANS
½ pound fresh cranberry beans, shelled
1 small onion, trimmed and halved
1 small carrot, trimmed
2 cloves garlic
Salt

FOR THE DRESSING
½ tsp finely grated peeled ginger
½ tsp finely grated lime zest
Freshly squeezed juice of 1 lime
2½ tsp soy sauce
2½ Tbsp Asian sesame oil
2½ tsp extra-virgin olive oil
7 drops Tabasco
2½ tsp sesame seeds, toasted
2½ tsp thinly sliced scallion, white part only

FOR THE SEAFOOD
3 Tbsp extra-virgin olive oil
24 littleneck clams, scrubbed and rinsed well
24 mussels, scrubbed and rinsed well
1 shallot, thickly sliced
2 sprigs thyme
¼ cup dry white wine
½ pound squid, cleaned, washed, body cut into
    ½-inch-wide rings (leave tentacles whole or
    cut in half if large)

FOR ASSEMBLY
4 oil-packed roasted red peppers, preferably
    piquillo, drained, seeded, and cut into 1-inch
    triangles
2 large tomatoes, peeled, seeded, and cut into
    1-inch triangles
6 large mint leaves, cut into thin strips
Salt and freshly ground pepper
1 lime, peeled, segmented, and finely diced

TO MAKE THE BEANS
Put the beans, onion, carrot, garlic, and 1 teaspoon salt in a medium saucepan and add enough water to cover. Bring to a boil, then simmer until the beans are tender but not splitting, 20 to 30 minutes. Discard the onion, carrot, and garlic. Cool the beans in their cooking liquid.

TO MAKE THE DRESSING
Whisk together the ginger, zest, juice, soy sauce, sesame oil, olive oil, Tabasco, sesame seeds, and scallion in a medium bowl.

TO MAKE THE SEAFOOD
Warm the olive oil in a shallow pot or deep skillet over medium heat. Add the clams, mussels, shallot, and thyme, and cook for 1 minute. Add the white wine; cover and cook until the shells begin to open, 2 to 3 minutes. Add the squid and cook, uncovered, for 2 to 3 minutes more. Discard the shallot, thyme, and any clams and mussels that haven't opened. When cool enough to handle, remove the clam and mussel meat. Discard the shells. Transfer the seafood to a bowl and keep warm. Strain the cooking liquid through a fine-mesh sieve and return it to the pot. Bring to a boil, and cook until the liquid is reduced to about ¼ cup, 4 to 6 minutes.

TO SERVE
Toss the warm seafood with the reduced liquid in a large bowl. Add the cranberry beans, dressing, piquillo peppers, tomatoes, and mint. Season to taste with salt and pepper and toss well. Spoon into a large serving bowl and sprinkle the diced lime on top.

Tsing Tao, a Chinese beer, keeps this dish casual, but if the goal is to dress it up, a Riesling "Norheimer Kirschheck" Spätlese, Weingut Donnhoff 2001 may be in order.

Lobster Roll Sandwich

Makes 4 servings

1 small carrot, coarsely grated
1 small stalk celery, peeled and coarsely grated
½ small fennel bulb, trimmed
    and coarsely grated
6 medium pink radishes, trimmed
    and coarsely grated
½ cup mayonnaise
1 Tbsp chopped cornichons
1 Tbsp small capers, rinsed, dried and chopped
1 Tbsp freshly squeezed lemon juice
1½ tsp Dijon mustard
1½ tsp finely chopped flat-leaf parsley
1½ tsp finely chopped chives
1½ tsp finely chopped tarragon leaves
6 drops Tabasco
Salt and freshly ground pepper
8 ounces cooked lobster meat (from two 1½-
    pound lobsters), cut into ½-inch chunks
Four 7- to 8-inch-long baguettes or good-quality
    hot-dog buns
4 thin slices prosciutto

Squeeze the carrot, celery, fennel, and radishes between your hands to remove the excess liquid;
transfer to a medium bowl. Add the mayonnaise,
cornichons, capers, lemon juice, mustard, parsley,
chives, tarragon, and Tabasco, and season with salt
and pepper; mix well to combine. Toss in the lobster chunks and stir until mixed well.

Cut the baguettes lengthwise in half (but do not
slice through completely). Open the baguettes like
a book. Line the top half of each baguette with a
slice of prosciutto and then spoon the lobster filling into the center. If not serving immediately,
wrap the sandwiches in parchment paper or plastic
wrap and refrigerate, or store in a well-chilled
portable cooler stocked with plenty of ice packs.

How to Cook a Lobster

Fill a tall stockpot (large enough to hold at least
1 lobster with the lid on) three-quarters full with
water and bring to a boil over high heat. Plunge
the live lobster(s) into the pot and cover immediately. Bring back to a boil and cook for 8 minutes;
remove the lobster and drain. When cool enough
to handle, crack the shells and remove the meat
from the claws (be sure to take out the piece of
cartilage near the "thumb" joint), knuckle, and tail.
Make a shallow incision lengthwise along the back
of the tail meat and remove the center vein. It is
important for lobsters to be alive until, or just before, they are cooked. Once lobsters die, the texture of the meat changes rapidly from firm to
mushy. Some people find it preferable to kill lobsters before boiling them. To do this quickly and
forcefully, insert a sharp heavy-duty chef's knife
lengthwise into the center of the lobster's head.
The lobster is killed instantaneously.

Variations

Pan-Asian Lobster Sandwich

On split sesame or semolina buns, layer lobster
chunks with slices of mango, peeled and seeded cucumber, crisp Bibb lettuce, mint and coriander
leaves, chopped peanuts, and a touch of wasabi.
Drizzle extra-virgin olive oil and freshly squeezed
lemon juice on top and season with salt and pepper.

*A beer such as Sierra Nevada Pale Ale is a barely bit-
ter thirst-quencher that will also act as a foil to the
lobster's sweetness in the basic roll. As for wine, the
Alsatian crisp 1998 Pinot Blanc from Domaine Trimbach matches the pan-Asian sandwich nicely, and a
well-founded white from Provence, such as the rich
1998 Bandol from Château de Pibarnon goes perfectly with the Niçoise-style variation.*

Lobster Pressed Sandwich à la Niçoise

Slice a large crusty round of country bread in half and lightly brush the cut sides with olive-tapenade paste. Layer the bottom half of the bread with lobster chunks, tomato slices, hard-cooked eggs, and arugula and basil leaves. Season everything liberally with extra-virgin olive oil, freshly squeezed lemon juice, and salt and pepper. Put the bread halves together, wrap in plastic wrap, and place on a tray. Weigh the tray down with another tray or a saucepan filled with soup cans or bags of rice and refrigerate for 4 hours to allow the juices and seasonings to penetrate the bread. Unwrap and cut into thick wedges before serving.

Shrimp Cakes

with Goat-Cheese Sauce

Makes 4 servings

FOR THE GOAT-CHEESE SAUCE
⅓ cup crème fraîche
⅔ cup heavy cream
¼ cup goat cheese, at room temperature
3 Tbsp chopped chives
1 Tbsp chopped shallots
1 tsp chopped garlic
2 Tbsp extra-virgin olive oil
2 Tbsp freshly squeezed lemon juice
2 Tbsp milk
Salt and freshly ground pepper

FOR THE SHRIMP CAKES
1 pound fingerling or Yukon Gold potatoes, peeled
1 pound extra-large or jumbo shrimp, peeled, deveined, and coarsely chopped
⅓ cup crème fraîche
5 cornichons, chopped
3 Tbsp chopped drained capers
¼ cup chopped celery
2 Tbsp finely chopped shallots
2 Tbsp chopped chives
1 Tbsp finely chopped radish
1 Tbsp Dijon mustard
1 Tbsp mayonnaise
1 Tbsp yellow mustard seeds
1 Tbsp chopped flat-leaf parsley
1 tsp finely chopped garlic
1 tsp chopped thyme leaves
1 tsp chopped tarragon leaves
Finely grated zest of ½ lemon
2 Tbsp extra-virgin olive oil, plus more for frying
1 Tbsp Banyuls vinegar or white-wine vinegar
Salt and freshly ground pepper
2 cups all-purpose flour
3 large eggs, lightly beaten
3 cups Panko (Japanese) bread crumbs

TO MAKE THE GOAT-CHEESE SAUCE
Mix together the crème fraîche, cream, goat cheese, chives, shallots, garlic, olive oil, lemon juice, and milk until well blended. Season with salt and pepper. *(The sauce can be made a few hours ahead and kept at room temperature.)*

TO MAKE THE SHRIMP CAKES
Center a rack in the oven and preheat to 350°F.

Put the potatoes in a large pot and add enough salted water to cover; bring to a boil. Cook until the potatoes are tender, 15 to 20 minutes. Drain; using a fork, coarsely crush the potatoes. Let cool slightly.

Mix together the potatoes, shrimp, crème fraîche, cornichons, capers, celery, shallots, chives, radish, mustard, mayonnaise, mustard seeds, parsley, garlic, thyme, tarragon, lemon zest, olive oil, and vinegar. Season with salt and pepper. Form the mixture into twelve ¾-inch-thick round cakes. Dip and coat each cake in the flour, then in the egg, and finally into the bread crumbs, making sure to coat them evenly and gently tapping off any excess.

Warm 3 tablespoons olive oil in a large nonstick skillet over medium heat. Cook 4 cakes until golden brown, 2 to 3 minutes on each side. Transfer the cakes to a shallow baking pan. Finish frying all the cakes, adding more olive oil as needed. Then bake for 5 minutes and drain on paper towels. Serve warm with the goat-cheese sauce.

A nice dry Riesling like the one made by Hermann J. Wiemer in New York's Finger Lakes region would pair well with the shrimp cakes, contributing a welcome element of acidity that spices up the dish. It is also light and minerally, echoing the flavors of the shrimp.

Steamed Red Snapper

in Bamboo Leaves

Makes 6 servings

FOR THE SNAPPER
7 to 8 bamboo leaves
Extra-virgin olive oil
1 orange
1 lemon
1 Meyer lemon
1 lime
2 stalks lemongrass, trimmed and outer leaves removed: 1 stalk finely chopped; 1 stalk crushed
2 Tbsp finely chopped cilantro leaves, stems reserved
1 Tbsp finely chopped flat-leaf parsley leaves, stems reserved
1 Tbsp finely chopped mint leaves, stems reserved
1 Tbsp finely chopped tarragon leaves, stems reserved
Two 1-inch pieces peeled ginger: 1 piece finely grated; 1 piece crushed
One 4-pound whole red snapper, cleaned
Salt and freshly ground pepper
1 bunch scallions, trimmed and chopped

FOR THE RICE AND THE HERB SALAD
1 Tbsp unsalted butter
Salt
1 cup wild rice
¾ cup jasmine or regular long-grain rice, rinsed well and drained
1 scallion, trimmed and chopped
1 clove garlic, finely chopped
One ¼-inch-thick slice peeled ginger, finely chopped
1 tsp salt
1 Thai peppercorn, crushed, or ½ tsp each whole white and black peppercorns, crushed
¼ cup vegetable oil
2 Tbsp soy sauce

1 Tbsp rice-wine vinegar
Finely grated zest of ½ orange
Finely grated zest of 1 lemon
Finely grated zest of 1 lime
½ bunch flat-leaf parsley, leaves only
½ bunch cilantro, leaves only
¼ bunch mint, leaves only
Freshly ground pepper

TO MAKE THE SNAPPER
Soak the bamboo leaves in cold water for 1 hour. (The leaves might need to be weighed down at first.) Remove the leaves from the water bath and pat dry. Brush both sides with olive oil; set aside.

Center a rack in the oven and preheat to 350°F.

Remove the zest from the orange, lemon, Meyer lemon, and lime in strips with a vegetable peeler. Cut the fruit into thin slices, set aside. Mix together the fruit zests; chopped lemongrass, cilantro, parsley, mint, and tarragon leaves; and grated ginger in a bowl. Season the fish with salt and pepper and rub the zest mixture over both sides, but not on the head. Place the leaves on a work surface, narrow ends facing up, slightly overlapping, to make a bed for the fish. Lay the snapper across the center of the leaves. Starting with the last leaf set down, lift up the ends of each leaf until they meet. Using toothpicks, secure each leaf as close to the fish as possible. Repeat until all the leaves are secured. Set aside.

Put the fruit slices; crushed lemongrass; cilantro, parsley, mint, and tarragon stems; crushed ginger; and scallions in the bottom of a steamer or fish poacher. Cover with water and bring to a boil. Place the fish on the steamer tray, making sure that it does not touch the boiling water; cover the pan. Bake until tender, 35 to 40 minutes.

To Make the Rice

Bring 2½ cups water, the butter, and ¾ teaspoon salt to a boil in a large deep saucepan. Mix in the wild rice; return to boil. Reduce the heat; cover and simmer about 30 minutes. Mix in the jasmine rice; cover and simmer until all the rice is tender and almost all the liquid is absorbed, about 18 minutes. Just before serving, fluff the rice with a fork.

To Make the Herb Salad

Put the scallion, garlic, ginger, 1 teaspoon salt, and crushed peppercorns in a small bowl. Pour the oil into a small saucepan and heat just until it begins to smoke. Stand back and carefully pour the hot oil over the scallion mixture. Stir well, then let rest for 2 minutes. Discard the garlic and ginger. Whisk in the soy sauce, vinegar, and citrus zests. Put the parsley, cilantro, and mint into a bowl. Add the scallion-oil mixture and toss to coat. Taste and season with salt and pepper if needed.

To Serve

Transfer immediately the fish (still wrapped in the bamboo leaves) to a large platter and bring to the table. Remove the toothpicks and unwrap the fish. Scrape off the herbs and citrus zest. Serve the fish with the rice and herb salad.

The flavors of this snapper get a nice lift from a highly aromatic wine like Viognier. Cold Heaven Winery in Santa Barbara makes a wonderful full-bodied version with floral tones that punch up the fish.

Grilled Tuna

with Rosemary-Fennel Coulis

Makes 4 servings

1 Tbsp balsamic vinegar

10 Tbsp extra-virgin olive oil

1 sprig thyme, leaves chopped

1 sprig rosemary, leaves chopped

1½ cloves garlic: 1 clove crushed; ½ clove
finely chopped

½ tsp fennel seeds

1 tsp crushed whole black peppercorns

Tabasco

Salt

Four 6- to 7-ounce tuna, salmon, or swordfish
steaks (1 inch thick)

3 small fennel bulbs, trimmed, and each cut into
8 wedges

Freshly squeezed juice of ½ lemon

2 small zucchini, cut on the diagonal into ⅓-inch-
thick slices

2 ounces oil-packed sun-dried tomatoes,
drained and diced

Freshly ground pepper

Vegetable oil

Balancing the richness of this dish calls for a well-structured, acidic wine like "Hildegard," a Pinot Gris-Pinot Blanc blend produced in the style of a Corton Charlemagne by Au Bon Climat winery in Santa Barbara. Its full body preserves a zestiness that melds well with the tuna's texture.

Combine the vinegar, 4 tablespoons olive oil, half of the thyme, half of the rosemary, the crushed garlic, fennel seeds, and crushed peppercorns. Season with Tabasco and salt. Coat the tuna steaks with the mixture and marinate in the refrigerator for at least 3 hours or overnight.

Bring a large pot of salted water to a boil. Add the fennel wedges and cook until tender but still firm, about 10 minutes. Using a slotted spoon, remove 16 of the fennel wedges; set aside and keep warm. Continue to cook the remaining fennel until very tender, about 5 minutes more. Transfer to a blender and add 1 tablespoon of the cooking liquid. Puree until slightly chunky. Add 3 tablespoons olive oil, 2 drops Tabasco, and the lemon juice, and puree until smooth. If the coulis is too thick, add cooking liquid. Season with salt and pepper. Strain through a fine-mesh sieve; set aside, and keep warm.

Warm the remaining 3 tablespoons olive oil in a small skillet over medium heat. Add the zucchini and cook, stirring, for 3 to 5 minutes. Add the rest of the thyme and rosemary, the chopped garlic, the reserved fennel wedges, and the sun-dried tomatoes. Season with salt and pepper. Continue to cook, stirring, until the zucchini is tender, about 5 minutes. Set aside and keep warm.

Prepare a very hot grill or stove-top griddle. Brush with vegetable oil and grill the tuna for 3 minutes on each side for rare steaks or 5 minutes on each side for medium-rare ones.

To Serve
Spoon the fennel coulis into the center of a warm serving platter. Place the vegetables on top and arrange the tuna steaks over them. Serve immediately.

Orange–Glazed Sea Bream

with Tomato, Pesto and Fennel

Makes 4 servings

2 bunches basil (about 3 ounces), leaves only, washed

4 cloves garlic: 2 cloves finely chopped; 2 cloves peeled

¾ cup extra-virgin olive oil

Salt and freshly ground pepper

8 medium plum tomatoes

3 Tbsp chopped onion

1 shallot, chopped

1 stalk celery, peeled, trimmed, and finely diced

1 leek, white and light-green parts only, finely diced, washed, and dried

Bouquet garni (1 sprig thyme, 1 sprig flat-leaf parsley, 1 bay leaf, tied with a strip of leek green)

1 Tbsp plus 1 tsp finely grated orange zest

16 baby fennel bulbs

2 sprigs thyme

Freshly squeezed juice of 3 oranges

Four 6-ounce sea bream fillets

Bring a large pot of salted water to a boil. Add the basil leaves and blanch until tender, 1 to 2 minutes. Drain and run cold running water over them to cool. Squeeze to remove the excess water. Put the basil, the whole garlic clove, and ¼ cup of the oil in a blender or food processor and puree until smooth. Season with salt and pepper. Transfer to an airtight container or cover with plastic wrap.

Bring a large pot of water to a boil. Cut a small X in the bottom of each tomato, add to the boiling water, and blanch for 10 seconds. Drain and run cold running water over them to cool. Peel, seed, and coarsely chop the tomatoes.

Warm 2 tablespoons of olive oil in a large skillet over medium heat. Add the onion, shallot, half of the chopped garlic, celery, leek, bouquet garni, and 1 teaspoon of the orange zest and cook, stirring, until the vegetables are soft but have no color, 5 to 6 minutes. Add the tomatoes and cook until the liquid has evaporated, 20 to 25 minutes. Season with salt and pepper; discard the bouquet garni. Transfer to a bowl and keep warm.

Wipe clean the inside of the skillet. Warm 2 tablespoons olive oil over medium heat. Add the fennel, the remaining 1 tablespoon orange zest, and 1 sprig of thyme; season with salt and pepper. Cook, stirring, for 2 to 3 minutes. Add enough water to cover and simmer until the fennel is tender, 15 to 20 minutes. Using a slotted spoon, transfer the fennel to a plate; keep warm. Put half of the fennel into a blender, add ¼ cup of the cooking liquid, the remaining chopped garlic, and 1 tablespoon olive oil; puree until smooth. Taste and season with salt and pepper if needed. Keep warm.

Cook the orange juice in a medium skillet over high heat until reduced to 3 tablespoons, or until it reaches a syrupy consistency.

Warm the remaining 3 tablespoons olive oil in a large skillet over medium-high heat. Season the fillets with salt and pepper and slip them into the pan, skin side down, with the garlic clove and remaining sprig of thyme. Cook for 3 minutes. Flip over and cook for another 3 minutes.

To Serve

Place a fillet and two fennel wedges on top of a spoonful of tomato compote in the center of each plate. Spoon the fennel coulis around the fish and drizzle on the basil puree and orange glaze.

White Hermitage, historically one of the best wines in France, is full bodied with nutty aromas and fairly low acidity—an exceptional choice keeping in mind the oiliness of the sea bream.

Meat, Poultry, and Side Dishes

This chapter encompasses a lot of traditional European fare, such as my Seed-Crusted Rack of Pork, a family heirloom that reminds me of my childhood. But many of the recipes also represent the contributions of foreign cultures to my cooking over the years, proof that it is possible to stay rooted in tradition while adopting new ingredients and techniques—half the fun of being a chef.

I have always enjoyed modernizing French standards like Peppered Côte de Boeuf and Duck à l'Orange; however, I am just as excited by the prospect of developing new classics, such as my Lamb Chops, whose fennel-and-cumin marinade and gingered-tomato and spiced-yogurt sauces are all derived from Middle Eastern flavors. The influence of American regional cuisine also finds its way into dishes like the Peanut-Crusted Pork Tenderloin, whose heritage is undeniably Southern. And then there's my Classic Hamburger, because what's more American than that? But of course, I have to impart it with a little Daniel, so, in addition to the basic recipe, I have included Asian-, North African—, and Indian-inspired variations.

Rounding out the chapter are side dishes—an Alsatian Potato Gratin, Spaghetti Squash with Sage, Creamy Polenta—fitting complements to an entrée or perhaps a main course on their own. And finally, for chilly winter nights, the country-food comforts of my Casual Cassoulet and Lamb Stew are wonderful and heart-warming, because sometimes the simplest meals are the most satisfying.

Classic Hamburger

and Three Variations

Makes 4 servings

FOR THE CLASSIC BURGER
1 Tbsp unsalted butter
1 small onion, finely chopped
Salt
1¼ pounds ground beef, preferably well-marbled shoulder and not too finely ground
2 ounces Gruyère or Emmenthal cheese, diced into ¼-inch cubes (optional)
2 Tbsp finely chopped flat-leaf parsley leaves
2 Tbsp Dijon mustard, plus more for serving
1 large egg, lightly beaten
¼ tsp each coarsely ground, lightly toasted white, black, pink, and green peppercorns
2 Tbsp extra-virgin olive oil
Eight ½-inch-thick slices sourdough bread
1 clove garlic, halved
4 leaves Boston lettuce
1 ripe, medium tomato, cut into ¼-inch-thick slices

Melt the butter in a small skillet over medium-low heat. Add the onion and season with salt. Cook, stirring, until the onion is tender and translucent, 5 to 7 minutes. Set aside to cool.

Combine the onion, ground beef, cheese, parsley, mustard, egg, and peppercorns in a medium bowl and season with salt; mix well. Form 4 round patties, each about 1 inch thick. *(Patties can be covered with plastic wrap and refrigerated up to 8 hours; remove from the refrigerator 30 minutes before cooking.)*

Center a rack in the oven and preheat to 375°F.

Warm 1 tablespoon olive oil in a large ovenproof skillet over high heat. When the oil begins to smoke slightly, add the patties, cook for 4 minutes on each side. Transfer the pan to the oven and cook for an additional 2 to 3 minutes for medium-rare burgers.

If barbecuing outdoors, put the patties on a hot grill and cook for 4 to 5 minutes on each side for medium-rare burgers.

Meanwhile, lightly brush the bread with the remaining tablespoon of olive oil. Grill or toast in a skillet until golden, about 2 minutes on each side. Rub the hot toasted bread with the garlic.

TO SERVE
Spread some mustard on a piece of toast and top with a burger, lettuce leaf, tomato slices, and another slice of toast.

FOR THE ASIAN BURGER
1¼ pounds ground pork
2 scallions, white part only, thinly sliced
1 clove garlic, finely chopped
1 tsp finely grated, peeled ginger
1 large egg, lightly beaten
4 tsp soy sauce
2 tsp milk
2 tsp all-purpose flour
Large pinch of hot-pepper flakes
Salt and freshly ground pepper
Mustard greens
Horseradish-spiked mayonnaise

Mix together the pork, scallions, garlic, ginger, egg, soy sauce, milk, flour, and hot-pepper flakes in a bowl, and season with salt and pepper. Cook as directed in the master recipe but increase the cooking time by 4 to 5 minutes on each side. Garnish the burgers with the mustard greens and mayonnaise.

FOR THE NORTH AFRICAN BURGER
1¼ pounds ground lamb
¼ cup coarsely chopped canned chickpeas, or 4 ounces feta cheese, broken into ¼-inch pieces
1 large egg, lightly beaten
4 tsp ketchup

2 tsp all-purpose flour
2 tsp milk
2 tsp Dijon mustard
¼ tsp crushed, toasted coriander seeds
Pinch of ground cinnamon or star anise
Salt and freshly ground pepper
Thinly sliced fennel
Roasted red pepper strips
Extra-virgin olive oil
Freshly squeezed lemon juice

Mix together the lamb, chickpeas, egg, ketchup, flour, milk, mustard, coriander, and cinnamon in a large bowl, and season with salt and pepper. Cook as directed in the master recipe. Garnish the burgers with fennel and roasted red pepper seasoned with olive oil, lemon juice, salt, and pepper.

FOR THE INDIAN BURGER
1 Tbsp unsalted butter
1 small red onion, finely chopped
Salt
1¼ pounds ground chicken or turkey, preferably
    a mix of light and dark meats
1 large egg, lightly beaten
¼ cup crushed salted peanuts
4 tsp mango chutney, plus more for serving
4 tsp shredded unsweetened coconut, toasted
3 Tbsp golden raisins, chopped
2 tsp all-purpose flour
1 tsp Madras curry powder
Pinch of cayenne
Freshly ground pepper
Lettuce leaves
Thinly sliced apple
Extra-virgin olive oil
Freshly squeezed lemon juice

Cook the onion as directed in the master recipe. Mix together the onion, chicken, egg, peanuts,

chutney, coconut, raisins, flour, curry powder, and cayenne, and season with salt and pepper. Cook as directed in the master recipe, but increase the cooking time by 4 to 5 minutes. Garnish the burgers with lettuce and thinly sliced apple seasoned with olive oil, lemon juice, salt, and pepper.

A hamburger is just not a hamburger without a glass of beer. The golden-hued Corona from Mexico, a smooth OB from Korea, and a Belgian Chimay ale all make excellent accompaniments, no matter which variation you choose.

Daniel's Casual Cassoulet

Makes 8 servings

FOR THE CASSOULET
2 Tbsp unsalted butter
2 Tbsp extra-virgin olive oil
One 4-pound Pekin duck, legs and breasts
   removed and split
1½ pounds lamb shoulder, cut into 8 pieces
8 Toulouse sausages or sweet Italian link sausages
Salt and freshly ground pepper
1 pound slab bacon, diced into 8 large cubes
2 large onions, diced into ½-inch cubes
4 large carrots, diced into ½-inch cubes
2 large stalks celery, peeled and diced into ½-inch
   cubes
1 head garlic, separated into cloves, peeled,
   and sliced
Bouquet garni (1 bay leaf, 4 sprigs flat-leaf parsley,
   and 3 sprigs thyme, tied with a strip of leek
   green)
2 Tbsp tomato paste
1 pound tomatoes, peeled, seeded, and diced into
   ½-inch cubes
2½ pounds cannellini beans (about 6 cups),
   pre-soaked in cold water for 8 to 12 hours
Piment d'Espelette or sweet paprika and cayenne

FOR THE TOPPING AND FINISHING
2 cups fresh bread crumbs
3 Tbsp coarsely chopped flat-leaf parsley leaves
6 cloves garlic, finely chopped
Salt and freshly ground pepper
6 Tbsp melted unsalted butter, melted duck fat,
   or vegetable oil

Center a rack in the oven and preheat to 400°F.

Melt the butter with the oil in a shallow 12-quart pot or Dutch oven over medium heat. Season the duck, lamb, and sausage with salt and pepper. Add to the pot, along with the bacon, and brown the meats evenly on all sides. Add the onions, carrots, celery, garlic, and bouquet garni, and cook stirring, for 10 minutes. Add the tomato paste and mix well. Add the tomatoes, beans, and 16 cups water; slowly bring to a boil. Cover the pot and bake until the beans are tender, 1 to 1½ hours. (Do not over-cook the beans; they will split.) After 45 minutes, check the cassoulet and if needed, add more water. Remove from the oven. Season to taste with salt, pepper, and piment d'Espelette.

Reduce the oven temperature to 350°F.

Combine the bread crumbs, parsley, and garlic in a mixing bowl and season with salt and pepper.

Sprinkle half the bread-crumb topping over the cassoulet and drizzle with half the melted butter. Bake uncovered for 15 to 20 minutes and remove from the oven. Using the back of a spoon, push the crust down into the liquid to moisten. Cover with the remaining bread-crumb topping and drizzle on the rest of the butter

Preheat the broiler. Broil the cassoulet, watching it closely, until the crust is golden brown, 5 to 7 minutes .

Such a rich, rustic dish calls for a wine that has ample body and tannic structure, like the famous Château Montus made from Tannat grapes. Also, in California's Livermore Valley, Ridge produces a terrific full-bodied wine with a Gamay aroma called Mataro.

Guinea Hen Casserole
with Morels, Fava Beans, and Fiddlehead Ferns

Makes 4 servings

½ pound fiddlehead ferns, cleaned and trimmed

1 cup shelled fresh fava beans (about 1½ pounds with pods)

2 Tbsp extra-virgin olive oil

One 2½- to 3-pound free-range guinea hen, cut into eight pieces

Salt and freshly ground pepper

½ pound morel mushrooms, stemmed, washed twice, and drained

½ pound new potatoes, scrubbed and halved

8 cloves garlic, unpeeled

4 shallots, halved, or 8 spring onions, trimmed

1 bay leaf

1 sprig thyme, leaves only, chopped

2 Tbsp unsalted butter

1 cup unsalted beef stock or low-sodium beef broth

2 Tbsp minced chives

Bring a large saucepan of water to a boil over high heat. Add the fiddlehead ferns and cook for 6 to 7 minutes. Add the fava beans and cook for 3 to 4 minutes more. Drain and run cold water over the ferns and favas to cool. Make a small incision in the skin of the favas with your thumbnail and pop out the beans. Discard the skins.

Center a rack in the oven and preheat to 375°F.

Warm the olive oil in a large cast-iron pot or roasting pan over high heat. Season the hen with salt and pepper. When the oil is hot, slip in the pieces, skin side down, and sear until golden brown, 5 to 7 minutes. Turn the pieces over and add the morels, potatoes, garlic, shallots, bay leaf, thyme, and butter, and season with salt and pepper. Cook, tossing, for 5 minutes. Slide the pan into the oven and roast for 25 to 30 minutes until the juices run clear when the hen is pierced.

Transfer the hen and the vegetables to a large bowl and keep warm. Place the pan over high heat on the stove; add the beef stock and reduce the liquid by half. Return the hen and vegetables to the pan and toss until heated through, 2 to 3 minutes. Sprinkle with the chives and serve family-style from the pan.

A rich Australian red with hints of cassis, chocolate, and walnut, Rosemount Estate's Shiraz would pair nicely with the guinea hen, as would an Argentine merlot from Bodega Weinert, whose big, flamboyant taste is also a bargain.

Lamb Stew

with Rosemary and Orange

Makes 6 servings

4 to 6 Tbsp extra-virgin olive oil

One 4-pound lamb shoulder, boned and cut into 1-inch chunks

Salt and freshly ground pepper

1 large onion, cut into ½-inch-thick wedges

4 small carrots, cut into ½-inch-thick slices

2 large turnips, peeled and diced into ½-inch cubes or 16 baby turnips, peeled and trimmed

1 large celery root, peeled and diced into ½-inch cubes

1 medium fennel bulb, trimmed and cut into 6 wedges

3 cloves garlic, coarsely chopped

1 tsp finely chopped rosemary leaves

One 3-inch cinnamon stick

¼ cup all-purpose flour

2 Tbsp tomato paste

1 tsp finely chopped flat-leaf parsley

Freshly squeezed juice of 1 orange

½ cup dry white wine

5 to 6 cups water or unsalted chicken stock

4 plum tomatoes, peeled, seeded, and cut into ½-inch cubes

½ tsp finely grated orange zest

Center a rack in the oven and preheat to 300°F.

Warm 2 tablespoons of olive oil in a Dutch oven or large pot over high heat. Season the lamb with salt and pepper. Sear the meat on all sides until golden brown, 10 to 15 minutes. Transfer to a plate. Add 2 tablespoons of olive oil to the pot and reduce the heat to medium-high. Add the onion, carrots, turnips, celery root, fennel, garlic, rosemary and cinnamon stick. Season with salt and pepper and cook, stirring, until the vegetables soften, 10 to 12 minutes. Add the lamb and cook, stirring, for 6 to 8 minutes, adding more olive oil if needed.

Sprinkle the flour on top and continue to cook, stirring, for 5 minutes. Stir in the tomato paste and parsley. Add the orange juice and wine and cook until the liquid is reduced by half. Add enough water to almost cover the lamb and vegetables; bring to a boil. Add the tomatoes and orange zest; cover the pot. Bake until the lamb is fork-tender, 60 to 75 minutes. Serve immediately.

The very affordable Dr. Cosimo Taurino's Notarpa-naro, a peppery Italian wine, is a great match. Another option comes from California: Infused with the penetrating aromas of spices and cassis, Ravenswood Zinfandel, Vintner's Blend, is also characterized by its smoked-meat and dried-fruit flavors.

Seed-Crusted Rack of Pork

with Cabbage-Cranberry Compote

Makes 4 servings

FOR THE CRUST

½ cup fresh bread crumbs

4 Tbsp unsalted butter, at room temperature

1 shallot, finely chopped

1 Tbsp finely chopped flat-leaf parsley leaves

1 Tbsp coarsely chopped pumpkin and
    sunflower seeds

1 Tbsp coarsely chopped walnuts and pine nuts

½ Tbsp coarsely chopped raisins

1 tsp flax seeds

Salt and freshly ground pepper

FOR THE COMPOTE

1 small head red cabbage (about 1 pound)

2 Tbsp unsalted butter

1 large onion, thinly sliced

2 apples, preferably Granny Smith or Macoun,
    peeled, cored, and each cut into eight wedges

1 cup fresh or frozen cranberries

½ cup red wine vinegar

Finely grated zest of 1 orange

½ cup freshly squeezed orange juice

½ Tbsp quatre-épices (four-spice) mix

Salt and freshly ground pepper

FOR THE ROASTED RACK OF PORK

One 2½-pound rack of pork (with 4 chops)

Salt and freshly ground pepper

3 Tbsp extra-virgin olive oil

1 medium carrot, chopped

1 medium onion, chopped

1 stalk celery, sliced

1 clove garlic, crushed

Bouquet garni (1 bay leaf, 1 sprig flat-leaf parsley,
    and 1 sprig thyme, tied with a strip of leek green)

2 Tbsp unsalted butter

¾ cup chicken stock or low-sodium chicken broth.

TO MAKE THE CRUST

Mix together the bread crumbs, butter, shallot, parsley, pumpkin and sunflower and flax seeds, walnuts and pine nuts, and raisins. Season with salt and pepper. Roll the butter mixture out between two pieces of parchment paper or plastic wrap into an 8-by-4-by-⅛ inch rectangle. Refrigerate until firm, about 2 hours.

TO MAKE THE COMPOTE

Discard the outer cabbage leaves. Halve the cabbage and cut out the core. Thinly slice the cabbage.

Melt the butter in a large skillet over medium-high heat. Add the onion and cook, until translucent, about 5 minutes. Add the cabbage, apples, and cranberries, and cook for 10 minutes. Deglaze with the vinegar and cook for 2 to 3 minutes. Add the orange zest and juice and quatre épices. Season with salt and pepper. Reduce the heat to medium-low and cook, stirring frequently, until the cabbage is tender, 40 to 45 minutes. Taste and season with salt and pepper if needed. Set aside and keep warm.

TO MAKE THE PORK

Center a rack in the oven and preheat to 350°F.

Season the pork with salt and pepper. Warm the olive oil in a large roasting pan over high heat on the stove. Cook, turning as needed, until the pork is well browned on all sides. Add the carrot, onion, celery, garlic, bouquet garni, and butter. Roast in the oven for 25 minutes, stirring the vegetables and basting the pork once or twice. Turn the rack over and roast, stirring and basting, for another 25 minutes.

Seghesio's "Old Vines" Zinfandel 2000 from Sonoma County is a rich red with the spicy overtones this dish requires.

Preheat the broiler. Place the seed crust over the pork. Press into the meaty side of the pork. Broil, watching closely, until the crust is golden brown, 3 to 4 minutes. Let the pork rest for 5 minutes before slicing into four chops. Discard the bouquet garni. Place the roasting pan over high heat on the stove and cook until the pan juices have reduced completely, about 3 minutes. Pour in the chicken stock, bring to a boil, and season with salt and pepper.

To Serve
Place a mound of the compote on each warm dinner plate. Spoon the vegetables and sauce over the compote and top with a pork chop. Serve immediately.

Peanut-Crusted Pork Tenderloin
with Southern-Style Vegetables

Makes 4 servings

For the Crust
⅓ cup milk

¼ cup shelled peanuts

⅓ cup fresh bread crumbs

2 Tbsp unsalted butter, at room temperature

5 to 6 drops Tabasco or 1 Tbsp whole-grain mustard

Salt and freshly ground pepper

For the Vegetables
2 medium sweet potatoes (about 1 pound), peeled, trimmed and cut lengthwise in half

Salt and freshly ground pepper

Quatre-épices (four-spice) mix

Two 3-inch cinnamon sticks, halved lengthwise

4 strips bacon

1 Tbsp plus 2 tsp extra-virgin olive oil

½ pound broccoli rabe, tough ends trimmed and coarse leaves removed

¼ pound okra, trimmed

For the Pork and Sauce
One 1½- to 2-pound pork tenderloin, trimmed

Salt and freshly ground pepper

½ tsp quatre-épices (four-spice) mix

½ tsp allspice

2 Tbsp extra-virgin olive oil

1 Tbsp unsalted butter

1 Serrano chile pepper, stemmed, halved, and seeded

¼ cup dry white wine

½ cup unsalted chicken stock or low-sodium chicken broth

For Serving
3 sprigs cilantro

2 sprigs flat-leaf parsley

To Make the Crust

Bring the milk to a boil in a small saucepan. Pour the hot milk over the peanuts in a bowl. Let sit for 20 minutes to soften the peanuts. Drain and chop the peanuts. Mix together the peanuts, bread crumbs, butter, and Tabasco in the same bowl; season with salt and pepper. Roll the peanut mixture out between two pieces of parchment paper into an 8-by-4-by-⅛-inch rectangle. Refrigerate until firm, about 2 hours.

To Make the Vegetables

Place the oven racks in the lower and upper third of the oven and preheat to 375°F.

Season the sweet potatoes with salt, pepper, and quatre épices. Place a cinnamon-stick half on the cut side of each sweet potato and wrap a bacon slice around the potato to secure the cinnamon stick. Drizzle ½ teaspoon olive oil over each potato, individually wrap in foil, and place on a baking sheet. Bake until tender, about 30 minutes.

Meanwhile, warm the remaining olive oil in a large oven-proof skillet over medium heat. Add the broccoli rabe and okra, season with salt, pepper, and quatre épices and cook, stirring, for 10 minutes. Bake until the okra is tender, 5 to 10 minutes.

To Make the Pork and Sauce

Center a rack in the oven and keep set at 375°F.

Season the tenderloin with salt, pepper, quatre épices, and allspice. On the stove, warm the oil in a large roasting pan over medium-high heat. When the oil is hot, add the pork to the pan and sear on all sides until browned, about 10 minutes. Add the butter to the pan; place in the oven and bake until an instant-read thermometer inserted into the middle of the pork reaches 140°F, about 10 minutes. Remove the pan from the oven.

Preheat the broiler. Place the crust on top of the pork. Broil, watching it closely, until the crust is golden brown, 3 to 4 minutes. Transfer the tenderloin to a cutting board; let rest for 5 minutes before slicing.

Meanwhile, drain the fat from the roasting pan and place the pan over high heat on the stove. Add the Serrano chile pepper and deglaze the pan with the wine; cook until reduced by half. Add the chicken stock and cook for 2 to 3 minutes. Taste and season with salt and pepper if needed.

To Serve

Place the broccoli rabe and okra in the center of a large warm platter. Arrange the sliced tenderloin on top of the vegetables. Remove the cinnamon sticks from the sweet potatoes and place the sweet potatoes around the tenderloin. Garnish with the cilantro and parsley and serve the sauce on the side.

The myriad spices in the peanut crust pair well with a rich, peppery Syrah. Qupé makes a great full-bodied, yet elegant version in the Central Coast of California.

Roasted Turkey Breast
with Endive, Apple, and Walnuts

Makes 6 servings

One 5- to 6-pound whole turkey breast, bone in
4 large bay leaves, halved lengthwise
8 strips bacon
Salt and crushed whole black peppercorns
3 Tbsp extra-virgin olive oil
1 Tbsp sherry vinegar
¼ cup walnut oil
10 medium Belgian endives, halved lengthwise, trimmed, and cut crosswise into ½-inch-thick pieces
2 medium Fuji apples, peeled, cored, and julienned
1 bunch flat-leaf parsley, leaves only
½ cup toasted walnuts
Freshly ground pepper

Center a rack in the oven and preheat to 425°F.

Debone the turkey breast; set the bones aside. Cut the breast in half and lay out horizontally, skin side up. Place 4 bay leaf halves crosswise along the center. Secure each bay leaf by wrapping a slice of bacon around the breast; tie with kitchen string. (The bay leaves must be completely covered to prevent them from burning.) Repeat with the second breast. Season both breasts with salt and crushed black pepper.

Warm the olive oil in a small roasting pan over high heat. When the oil is hot, add the turkey to the pan, skin side down, and brown for about 5 minutes. Turn the breasts over and cook until evenly browned, about 15 minutes more. Remove from the pan, pour off the fat, and add the bones. Arrange the breasts, skin side down, on top of the bones. Bake for 20 minutes. Turn over and bake until an instant-read thermometer inserted into the center of a breast reaches 150°F, about 20 minutes more. Transfer to a warm platter and keep warm.

Discard the bones and skim off the fat from the pan juices. Put the roasting pan on the stove, add ½ cup water, and bring to a boil. Reduce the liquid, stirring and scraping, until 2 tablespoons remain. Strain through a fine-mesh sieve into a medium bowl and whisk in the sherry vinegar and walnut oil.

Toss together the endive, apple, parsley, and walnuts in a large bowl and season with salt and ground pepper. Lightly coat the salad with the vinaigrette.

To Serve
Carefully remove the kitchen string and bay leaves from the turkey. Arrange the salad on a large platter and top with the breasts for carving tableside. Drizzle the remaining vinaigrette over everything.

Either a red Zinfandel or a cider would serve as a lively counterpart to the roasted turkey breast. George Hornsby's draft cider or a cider from the French brewery Manoir de Kinkiz is a classic with a multilayered flavor.

Peppered Côte de Boeuf
with Pommes Pont Neuf and Watercress Salad

Makes 2 servings

FOR THE POTATOES
2 large Idaho baking potatoes (¾ to 1 pound each)
Peanut oil for frying
1 Tbsp minced chives
1 tsp finely grated fresh horseradish
Salt and freshly ground pepper

FOR THE WATERCRESS SALAD
2 tsp Dijon mustard
2 tsp sherry vinegar
2 Tbsp extra-virgin olive oil
Salt and freshly ground pepper
1 bunch watercress, tough stems removed,
    washed, and dried
2 medium white mushrooms, stems removed and
    caps thinly sliced

FOR THE BEEF
4 beef-marrow bones (each 2 inches long)
3 Tbsp unsalted butter
1 small onion, finely chopped
Salt and freshly ground pepper
2 Tbsp red-wine vinegar
¼ cup fresh bread crumbs
1 Tbsp finely chopped flat-leaf parsley leaves
1 Tbsp extra-virgin olive oil
One 2-pound bone-in rib-eye steak, trimmed of all
    fat and tied
1 Tbsp crushed whole black peppercorns
1 shallot, finely chopped
2 Tbsp cognac or brandy
½ cup unsalted beef stock or low-sodium beef
    broth
1 Tbsp Dijon mustard
Fleur de sel or coarse sea salt, for serving

TO MAKE THE POTATOES
Peel the potatoes and cut into thick 2½-by-½-by-½-inch rectangles. Put the logs into a bowl and cover with cold water. Refrigerate for 2 hours.

Pour 3 to 4 inches of peanut oil into a deep pot and heat to 300°F as measured on a deep-fat thermometer. Drain the potatoes well, pat them dry, and slip them into the oil. Blanch until they are nearly tender but not browned, 7 to 10 minutes. Scoop out of the pot and drain on a paper-towel-lined plate.

When ready to serve, heat the oil to 375°F. Lower in the blanched potatoes and cook until crisp and golden on the outside, about 5 minutes. Scoop the potatoes from the oil and drain on clean paper towels. Toss with the chives, horseradish, salt, and pepper.

TO MAKE THE WATERCRESS SALAD
Whisk together the mustard and sherry vinegar in a medium bowl. Still whisking, drizzle in the olive oil to emulsify; season with salt and pepper. Before serving, toss the watercress and mushrooms with the dressing.

TO MAKE THE BEEF
Bring a medium pot of water to a boil. Scoop the marrow out of the bones and add it to the pot; discard the bones. Blanch the marrow for just 15 seconds, remove from the water, and set aside to cool. Cut the marrow into ¼-inch cubes, put into a medium bowl, and refrigerate.

Melt 1 tablespoon of the butter in a small skillet over medium-low heat. Add the onion, season with salt and pepper and cook, stirring, until the onion is tender but not browned, 5 to 7 minutes. Pour the vinegar into the pan and let it boil until no liquid is left. Remove from heat and set aside to cool.

Add the sautéed onion to the marrow and stir in the bread crumbs and parsley. Season with salt and pepper, cover and refrigerate.

Center a rack in the oven and preheat to 400°F.

Melt 1 tablespoon of the butter with the olive oil in a large ovenproof pan over high heat. Season the steak on all sides with salt and crushed peppercorns. Add the beef to the pan. Brown for 8 to 10 minutes before turning over and browning the other side for 8 to 10 minutes. Transfer the pan to the oven and roast about 15 minutes or until an instant-read thermometer reaches 135° to 140°F (for medium rare), basting every 5 minutes. Remove from the oven and transfer the steak to a warm platter or cutting board to rest while you prepare the jus.

Preheat the broiler.

Pour off all but about 1 tablespoon of the fat from the pan. Add the shallot to the pan and over medium-low heat, cook, stirring, for 3 to 4 minutes; pour in the cognac. Increase the heat to high and cook until all the liquid has evaporated. Add the beef stock and bring to a boil. Boil for 1 minute and remove from heat. Whisk in the mustard, the remaining tablespoon of butter, and any meat juices accumulated. Season with salt and pepper and strain the jus through a fine-mesh sieve into a warm sauceboat.

Remove the string from the beef. Return the beef to the same pan and top with the marrow crust. Place under the broiler until the marrow begins to melt and the bread crumbs brown lightly, 3 to 4 minutes.

To Serve
Sprinkle the marrow crust with fleur de sel or coarse sea salt and cut the steak into ½-inch-thick slices.

Arrange on a warm platter (or on two warm plates) with a stack or two of crisscrossed potato logs and some greens. Spoon the jus over the meat and serve immediately.

Two options are the Joseph Phelps 1997 Napa Valley Cabernet Sauvignon and the 1996 Côte Rôtie Brune et Blonde from Etienne Guigal.

Duck à l'Orange

Makes 4 servings

One 5-pound Muscovy or Pekin duck
Salt and freshly ground pepper
4 blood oranges: 2 juiced; 2 cut into quarters
4 cloves garlic, thinly sliced
1 sprig thyme
8 spring onions, trimmed or 2 small onions,
    thinly sliced
2 medium celery roots (½ pound each), peeled,
    cut into ½-inch-thick slices, quartered, and
    reserved in an ice-water and lemon-juice bath
2 bunches kale, Swiss chard, or mustard greens
    (about 1 pound), stems and tough center veins
    removed, washed, dried, and cut into ½-inch-
    wide strips
2 Tbsp sugar
¼ tsp whole black peppercorns, cracked
Finely grated zest of 1 large orange
¼ cup Grand Marnier or other orange-flavored
    liqueur
1 cup unsalted chicken stock or low-sodium
    chicken broth
Freshly squeezed juice of 1 large orange
1 tsp sherry vinegar
1 Tbsp unsalted butter or extra-virgin olive oil

A lush, round, medium-bodied red wine—a young Merlot from California or Bordeaux, for instance—will accent the duck's richness, while its spice will pair well with the glazed-orange sauce. The Château d'Aiguilhe, Bordeaux-Côtes de Castillon 2001, is a good bet.

Center a rack in the oven and preheat to 400°F.

Season the duck inside and out with salt and pepper. Tie the legs together and place the bird, breast side up, in a large roasting pan. Roast for 25 minutes.

Combine the blood-orange juice, garlic, and thyme in a bowl and pour over the duck. Scatter the onions, celery root, kale, and blood-orange segments around the duck; roast until an instant-read thermometer inserted into the leg reaches 140° to 150°F, about 25 minutes more.

Transfer the duck to a rack set over a large plate and let rest. Discard the blood-orange segments; transfer the vegetables to a bowl and keep warm. Skim off the fat from the roasting pan. Place the pan over medium heat. Add the sugar, cracked peppercorns, and orange zest, and cook for a few minutes, scraping up the bits in the pan.

Flambé by carefully adding the Grand Marnier and slowly tilting the pan toward the flame so the liqueur ignites. (If using an electric stove, use a long match.) When the flames subside, add the chicken stock, orange juice, vinegar, and butter, and cook, stirring and scraping up the browned bits, until the sauce has slightly thickened, 2 to 3 minutes. Taste and season with salt and pepper if needed.

To Serve

Separate the legs from the body and carve the duck breast into thin slices. Place the vegetables in the center of a large platter. Arrange the sliced duck breast and the legs on top of the vegetables. Spoon the sauce around the dish and serve immediately.

Marinated Lamb Chops
with Two Sauces

Makes 4 servings

FOR THE LAMB

1 Tbsp coriander seeds, finely crushed or ground
1 Tbsp fennel seeds, finely crushed or ground
1½ tsp ground cumin
1 small dried chile, seeded and finely chopped
2 cloves garlic, sliced
2 sprigs mint, leaves chopped
2 sprigs thyme, leaves chopped
¼ cup extra-virgin olive oil
Twelve 3-ounce lamb-rib chops (1 inch thick), fat trimmed and bone cut to 2 inches
Salt and freshly ground pepper

FOR THE GINGERED-TOMATO SAUCE

2 Tbsp extra-virgin olive oil
1 Tbsp finely chopped peeled ginger
1 shallot, finely chopped
6 beefsteak tomatoes, cored and roughly chopped
Salt and freshly ground pepper

FOR THE SPICED-YOGURT SAUCE

1 cup Greek or plain yogurt
1 Tbsp freshly squeezed lemon juice
2 sprigs mint, leaves very thinly sliced
1 clove garlic, finely chopped and mashed into puree
Salt and freshly ground pepper

FOR THE CRISPY SALAD

3 Tbsp extra-virgin olive oil
1 Tbsp freshly squeezed lemon juice
4 hearts of romaine, trimmed and leaves separated
2 fennel bulbs, trimmed and thinly sliced
10 radishes, trimmed and thinly sliced
½ English cucumber, thinly sliced
Salt and freshly ground pepper

TO MAKE THE LAMB

Put the coriander and fennel seeds, the ground cumin, and chile into a small skillet and toast over high heat until very fragrant. Set aside ⅛ teaspoon of the toasted spice mixture for the yogurt sauce.

Stir together the remaining spice mixture, garlic, mint, thyme, and olive oil in a large baking dish. Add the lamb; toss to coat with the marinade, cover, and refrigerate overnight.

TO MAKE THE GINGERED-TOMATO SAUCE

The next day, warm the olive oil in a large deep skillet over medium-high heat. Add the ginger and shallot and cook until soft but not colored. Reduce the heat to low; add the tomatoes, and cook until very soft, about 45 minutes, crushing the tomatoes with the back of a fork as they cook. Season with salt and pepper; set aside and keep warm.

TO MAKE THE SPICED-YOGURT SAUCE

Stir together the yogurt, lemon juice, mint, garlic, and the reserved ⅛ teaspoon spice mixture until blended. Season with salt and pepper. If the mixture is too thick, add a little water. Transfer to a serving bowl; set aside.

TO MAKE THE CRISPY SALAD

Whisk together the olive oil and lemon juice in a small bowl. Combine the romaine, fennel, radishes, and cucumber in a large bowl. Cover and refrigerate.

The meat's potent flavors demand a Syrah-based wine with smooth, supple tannins and unadulterated oomph, such as Fattoria di Manzano's Podere Il Bosco 1998 and the Villa Pillo 1999, both Tuscan Syrahs. For a fuller taste, try the spicy 1999 Primitivo di Manduria from Felline, also an Italian wine.

Remove the lamb from the marinade. Pat dry, cover with plastic wrap, and bring to room temperature.

Prepare a very hot grill and brush with vegetable oil. Season the lamb with salt and pepper and grill for 3 to 5 minutes on each side for medium rare chops.

To Serve
Rewhisk the lemon dressing. Drizzle over the salad, season with salt and pepper, and toss to coat. Place three lamb chops and some salad on each dinner plate. Serve the sauces separately.

Roasted Chicken
with Grapes, Artichokes, and a Chicory Salad

Makes 4 servings

FOR THE CHICKEN

One 3- to 3½-pound organic free-range chicken, cleaned, neck and liver reserved

4 sage leaves, stems cut off and reserved

1 Tbsp unsalted butter, at room temperature

Salt and freshly ground pepper

2 Tbsp extra-virgin olive oil

16 medium Jerusalem artichokes (peeled just before using)

1 head garlic, split crosswise

2 shallots, halved

20 pearl onions, peeled and trimmed

1 Tbsp sugar

1 cup dry white wine

1½ cups unsalted chicken stock or low-sodium chicken broth

1 cup seedless red grapes

FOR THE SALAD

Salt and freshly ground pepper

1 Tbsp extra-virgin olive oil

1 shallot, finely chopped

2 Tbsp sherry vinegar

2 Tbsp walnut oil

2 heads frisée, white part only, washed and dried

4 ounces mâche (lamb's lettuce), trimmed

1 cup homemade or store-bought garlic croutons

TO MAKE THE CHICKEN

Place a medium roasting pan in the oven and preheat to 425°F.

A hearty dish like this calls for a medium-bodied, spicy Pinot Noir from California's Central Coast, like Au Bon Climat 2000, whose muted cherry and earth overtones and long, sweet finish will bring out the flavors of the pearl onion and grape garnish.

Separate the chicken wings at the second joint; chop the neck bone into 3 pieces, reserve. Gently separate the skin from each breast and tuck a sage leaf underneath. Repeat with the legs. Smear the butter over the skin and generously season the chicken inside and out with salt and pepper. Truss with kitchen string.

Remove the pan from the oven and coat the bottom with olive oil. Place the neck and wing joints in the pan and place the chicken on top. Roast for 10 minutes, basting twice. Add the Jerusalem artichokes, garlic, shallots, and reserved sage stems to the pan, season with salt and pepper, and roast for 10 minutes more, basting twice.

Reduce the oven temperature to 400°F. Toss the pearl onions with the sugar and a bit of salt and add them to the pan. Roast the chicken until the juices run clear when a thigh is pierced with a knife or an instant-read thermometer reaches 180°F, 15 to 20 minutes more. Transfer to a board and remove the string. Place the chicken on a large serving platter and keep warm.

Skim the fat from the pan and place the pan on the stove. Add the wine and reduce over high heat until it has almost evaporated. Add the chicken stock and grapes and cook for about 2 minutes. Using a slotted spoon, transfer the artichokes, onions, and grapes to the platter and arrange around the chicken. Strain the remaining liquid through a fine-mesh sieve into a sauceboat, reserving 2 tablespoons of the pan sauce for the salad. After carving the chicken, drizzle each portion with some sauce.

TO MAKE THE SALAD

Season the reserved chicken liver with salt and pepper. Warm the olive oil in a small skillet over high heat. Add the liver and cook, stirring, for 1 minute. Add the shallots and cook for another minute. Deglaze the pan with the sherry vinegar and reduce by half.

Transfer the liver-shallot mixture to a salad bowl. Make a vinaigrette by crushing the livers with a fork, then stirring in the walnut oil and reserved pan sauce until mixed well. Season with salt and pepper. Add the frisée, mâche, and croutons and toss well.

Roasted Venison
with Date Sauce and Root Vegetables

Makes 6 servings

FOR THE SPICE MIXTURE
6 whole star anise
1¾ tsp ground cinnamon
¾ tsp freshly grated nutmeg

FOR THE MARINADE
1 tsp finely grated orange zest
½ cup freshly squeezed orange juice
2 Tbsp extra-virgin olive oil
2 cloves garlic, crushed
1 sprig thyme
¼ tsp whole black peppercorns
Eight 8-ounce venison T-bone steaks

FOR THE DATE SAUCE
¾ pound fresh dates or ½ pound dried dates
2 cups freshly squeezed orange juice
2 Tbsp sherry vinegar
1 clove garlic
1 sprig thyme
½ tsp finely grated orange zest
½ tsp salt

FOR THE GARNISH
2 tsp freshly squeezed lemon juice
3 medium turnips, peeled and quartered
3 salsify roots, peeled, trimmed, and cut into
    1½-by-¼-by-¼-inch sticks
1 small celery root, peeled, trimmed, cut into
    ½-inch-thick slices, and quartered
Zest of ½ navel orange, removed in strips with
    a vegetable peeler
2 Tbsp extra-virgin olive oil
6 shallots, peeled and halved
1 bunch Muscat grapes, peeled
1 clove garlic
1 sprig thyme
Salt and freshly ground pepper

18 icicle radishes, cleaned, and greens removed
½ cup unsalted chicken stock or low-sodium
    chicken broth

FOR THE VENISON
Salt and coarsely ground black pepper
2 Tbsp extra-virgin olive oil

TO MAKE THE SPICE MIXTURE
Finely grind the star anise; combine with the cinnamon and nutmeg. Set aside.

TO MAKE THE MARINADE
Mix together the orange zest and juice, olive oil, 2 teaspoons of the ground spice mixture, garlic, thyme, and peppercorns in a shallow pan, then roll the venison in the marinade to coat. Cover the pan tightly with plastic wrap and refrigerate for at least 4 hours, or preferably overnight, turning the meat a few times.

TO MAKE THE DATE SAUCE
Put the dates in a bowl and cover with warm water. Let stand until the skins loosen, 15 to 20 minutes. Peel and pit the dates and put them in a small pot. Add the orange juice, vinegar, 1 teaspoon of the ground-spice mixture, garlic, thyme, orange zest, and salt. Bring to a simmer over medium heat, and poach the dates until they are quite tender and resemble a compote, about 30 minutes. Discard the garlic and thyme. Put the dates and their poaching liquid into a food processor or blender and puree until smooth. Taste and season with salt if needed. (*The sauce may be made in advance, kept in the refrigerator, and reheated when ready to use.*)

TO MAKE THE GARNISH
Sprinkle the lemon juice over the turnips, salsify, and celery root in a bowl, tossing to coat.

Cut the orange zest into very thin long strips. Bring a small pot of water to a boil, add the zest, and boil for 2 minutes. Drain the zest and set aside to cool.

Warm the olive oil in a large skillet over medium heat. Add the turnips, salsify, celery root, orange zest, ¼ teaspoon of the ground-spice mixture, shallots, grapes, garlic, and thyme, and season with salt and pepper. Cook for 5 minutes. Add the radishes and cook for 5 minutes more. Add the chicken stock; reduce the heat, cover and braise, until the turnips and celery root are tender, 12 to 15 minutes. Uncover and gently toss the vegetables until all the liquid evaporates. Taste and season with salt and pepper if needed. Set aside and keep warm.

To Make the Venison
Center a rack in the oven and preheat to 350°F.

Remove the venison from the marinade; discard the marinade. Pat the meat dry with paper towels and season with salt, pepper, and the remaining ground-spice mixture. Warm the olive oil in a roasting pan over high heat on the stove. When the oil is very hot, add the meat to the pan and sear on all sides until golden brown, 1½ to 2 minutes on each side. Roast in the oven for approximately 20 minutes for medium-rare steaks, rotating the medallions occasionally. Remove the venison from the pan and let rest for 4 minutes.

Preheat the broiler. Brush the date sauce over the venison. Broil until the date sauce is hot, 2 to 3 minutes.

To Serve
Place the vegetables in the center of a warm platter. Arrange the venison on top of the vegetables. Serve the remaining date sauce on the side.

Balance the fruity spiced-date sauce with the 2000 Swanson Sangiovese, a Napa Valley red with a spicy nose and a dry finish. Another possibility is the 2000 Prieuré Saint-Jean de Bébian, another red, from the Coteaux du Languedoc in the south of France, which has a very ripe Chateauneuf-du-Pape-like style and flavor.

Alsatian Potato Gratin

Makes 10 side-dish servings or 6 main-dish servings

1 Tbsp extra-virgin olive oil

1 medium onion, thinly sliced

2 cloves garlic, finely chopped

Salt and freshly ground pepper

2 medium carrots (about ½ pound), thinly sliced

1 cup unsalted chicken stock or low-sodium chicken broth

½ head Savoy cabbage (about 1 pound), leaves separated and center veins removed

8 strips bacon

2 pounds Yukon Gold potatoes, peeled and thinly sliced crosswise

1 Tbsp unsalted butter, cut into small pieces

2 sprigs thyme

1 bay leaf

5 juniper berries

The dark-fruit and earthy aromas of an Oregon Pinot Noir like Cristom "Jefferson Cuvée" would echo the bacon and be generally well-suited to the richness of this dish.

Warm the olive oil in a large skillet over medium heat. Add the onion and garlic, and season with salt and pepper. Cook until the onion is translucent, 6 to 7 minutes. Add the carrots and ¼ cup of the chicken stock; cover. Reduce the heat to low and cook for 5 minutes. Uncover and cook for about 2 minutes. Remove from the heat and let cool.

Prepare an ice-water bath in a large bowl. Bring a large pot of salted water to a boil. Add the cabbage leaves and blanch until tender, 4 to 5 minutes. Using tongs, transfer the leaves to the ice-water bath. When cool, drain on paper towels.

Center a rack in the oven and preheat to 400°F.

Brush a 12-by 9-by-2-inch oval ovenproof serving dish with olive oil. Toss together the onions and carrots. Arrange 4 bacon strips diagonally in the bottom of the prepared dish and cover with half the potatoes slices, tightly overlapped. Season with salt and pepper and cover with half of the onion-carrot mixture. Top with the cabbage leaves and then the remaining onion-carrot mixture, seasoning each layer with salt and pepper. Add the rest of the potatoes and bacon. Season with salt and pepper. Pour the remaining ¾ cup chicken stock over the dish, dot evenly with the butter, and decorate with the thyme, bay leaf, and juniper berries.

Cut a piece of parchment paper the size of the dish and rub with olive oil. Place the paper, oil side down, on top of the gratin. Bake until the potatoes are tender and lightly browned, 60 to 75 minutes. Serve immediately.

Spaghetti Squash

with Sage

Makes 4 to 6 servings

2 Tbsp extra-virgin olive oil

¼ pound country-style bacon, diced into ¼-inch cubes (optional)

1 cup thinly sliced white onion

2 cloves garlic, thinly sliced

2 sprigs sage, stemmed and coarsely chopped, plus a few more sprigs for serving

2 medium spaghetti squash (about 2 to 3 pounds each), halved lengthwise and seeded

1 Tbsp unsalted butter

Salt and freshly ground pepper

Center a rack in the oven and preheat to 350°F.

Warm the olive oil in a large roasting pan over medium heat on the stove. Add the bacon and cook until lightly browned. Drain off half the fat. Add the onion, garlic, and sage, tossing to combine. Place the squash halves on top, cut side down, and cover the pan with foil. Bake until tender, 50 to 60 minutes.

Using a fork, scrape out the pulp in long strands. Return the pulp to the roasting pan. Add the butter, season with salt and pepper and toss to combine.

To Serve

Decorate with a few sprigs of sage and serve immediately.

Butternut Squash Gratin

Makes 4 to 6 servings

4 cups milk
1 small butternut squash (about 1 pound), peeled, seeded, and cut into 1½- to 2-inch chunks
1 tsp sugar
4 sage leaves
1 bay leaf
1 clove garlic
Salt and freshly ground white pepper
¾ cup heavy cream
½ cup coarsely grated Gruyère cheese

Center a rack in the oven and preheat to 350°F.

Bring the milk to a simmer in a large saucepan over medium heat. Add the squash, sugar, sage leaves, bay leaf, and garlic, and season with salt and pepper. Cook until the squash is tender, 30 to 40 minutes. Drain and transfer to an 8-inch-square baking dish. Pour in the heavy cream and sprinkle with the cheese. Bake until the cream has reduced to a thick sauce, 20 to 25 minutes.

Preheat the broiler. Broil the gratin, watching it closely, until the cheese is golden brown, 3 to 4 minutes. Serve immediately.

Yogurt Rhubarb
and Lime Dressing

Makes 4 to 6 servings

1 small stalk rhubarb, trimmed and thinly sliced
1 tsp honey
1 whole star anise
Finely grated zest and freshly squeezed juice of 1 lime
One 6-ounce container low-fat plain yogurt
4 drops Tabasco
Salt and freshly ground pepper
1 Tbsp sesame seeds, toasted

Bring ¼ cup water, rhubarb, honey, star anise, and lime zest to a boil in a small saucepan over medium heat. Cook until the rhubarb is very soft, 2 to 3 minutes. Let the mixture cool and discard the star anise. Strain through a sieve.

Whisk together the rhubarb coulis, yogurt, lime juice, and Tabasco in a small bowl; season with salt and pepper.

To Serve
Spoon the dressing over cold steamed asparagus, romaine lettuce, or a vegetable salad, and sprinkle the sesame seeds on top.

Creamy Polenta

with Porcini, Parmesan, and Oregano

Makes 4 servings

4 thin slices prosciutto or ham (optional)

3 Tbsp extra-virgin olive oil

1 pound porcini mushrooms, cleaned, trimmed, and cut into ¼-inch-thick slices

1 Tbsp finely chopped oregano leaves

Salt and freshly ground white pepper

2 large shallots, finely chopped

2 cloves garlic, finely chopped

1 Tbsp flat-leaf parsley leaves, finely chopped

3 cups unsalted chicken or vegetable stock or low-sodium chicken or vegetable broth

2¾ cups milk

1 cup instant polenta

¼ cup finely grated fresh Parmesan cheese

3 Tbsp unsalted butter

If using the prosciutto, center a rack in the oven and preheat to 250°F.

Line a baking sheet with parchment paper and arrange the prosciutto on top. Bake until crisp and dried, 45 minutes to 1 hour. Remove from the oven and set aside.

Warm the olive oil in a large skillet over high heat. Add the porcini and oregano and season with salt and pepper. Brown lightly, tossing frequently, for 4 to 6 minutes. Reduce the heat to medium and add the shallots, garlic, and parsley. Cook, stirring, for 2 minutes more. Remove from heat.

Combine the stock and milk in a medium saucepan. Season with salt and pepper and bring to a boil. Reduce the heat until the liquid just simmers; add the polenta in a fine stream, whisking constantly. Cook, stirring regularly with a wooden spoon, until the polenta has the consistency of loose mashed potatoes, 5 to 10 minutes. Remove from heat, stir in the Parmesan and butter; taste and season with salt and pepper if needed. *(The polenta can be prepared up to half an hour before serving and kept warm in the top of a double boiler set over simmering water. Press a piece of plastic wrap against the surface to prevent a skin from forming.)*

To Serve

Divide the polenta among four warm shallow bowls or soup plates. Spoon the reserved porcini and some of their cooking liquid over it and garnish with the dried prosciutto.

Breads and Desserts

Because they are created from relatively few ingredients, breads and desserts require a level of precision other recipes don't often demand. Measurements must be exact, ingredients must be consistent, and, with breads in particular, enough time must be allotted for the dough to rise—and sometimes rise again. But despite their exacting nature, breads and desserts are well worth the effort. After all, what's more comforting than a sugary treat or the intoxicating smell of freshly baked bread?

The Mini Baguettes and Butter Balls included here are the same as those we serve at DANIEL, so you can bring a little of the restaurant into your own home. There's also a recipe for sandwich buns, along with suggestions for fillings, that will impress even the pickiest picnicker.

As for dessert, whether you're celebrating the New Year with a Pineapple-and-Coconut Givré or saluting the Fourth of July with a Frozen Strawberry Soufflé, dinner should end on a sweet and lasting note. And, as with the other recipes in this book, the goal of maintaining a balanced relationship between flavors and textures stands. The cinnamon crunch of a flaky sacristain tempers the smooth rum-infused chocolate custard in Pot de Crème. Peppercorns give the Spiced Chocolate Soup a scintillating tang. Even something as simple and comforting as rice pudding can become an exotic treat with its Japanese-inspired green-tea accent.

In addition to the soup and pot de crème, chocolate lovers have cake and mousse to choose from, as well as chocolate-pistachio crêpes and three delectable ice creams. And because dessert brings out the kid in all of us, I've included a trio of cupcakes as well as my take on Chamonix à l'Orange, a sentimental reinvention of the candy-shortbread I loved as a child in France.

Speck Ham and Sage Boules

Makes 2 loaves

1 tsp extra-virgin olive oil
½ pound speck ham or prosciutto,
    cut into ¼-inch cubes
1 tsp fennel seeds
1 tsp coriander seeds
6 sprigs sage, leaves only
3 sprigs savory, leaves only
5 sprigs thyme, leaves only
1 package active dry yeast
3 Tbsp lukewarm water (105°–115°F)
2⅓ cups bread flour
1¼ cups pumpernickel or rye flour
¼ cup whole-wheat flour
1 Tbsp salt
1 bottle (12 ounces) Guinness beer, at room
    temperature
Cornmeal

Warm the olive oil in a small skillet over medium-high heat. Add the ham and cook for 1 minute. Add the fennel seeds, coriander seeds, sage, savory, and thyme, and cook 2 more minutes. Transfer to a paper-towel-lined plate and let cool. *(Can be made up to a day ahead and kept covered in the refrigerator.)*

Stir together the yeast and warm water in a small bowl and let stand until creamy, about 5 minutes. In the bowl of a mixer fitted with a dough hook, add the bread, pumpernickel and whole-wheat flours, salt, yeast mixture, and beer. Mix on low speed until the dough comes together, about 3 minutes.

Increase the speed to high and mix for 8 to 10 minutes. (Keep an eye on your mixer; it may shake on the counter as the dough becomes more elastic.)

Stop to check the dough: Wet your fingers and pull off a small piece. Stretch the dough between your fingers. It should be shiny, elastic, and smooth and should not break apart. Also check the inside of the mixer bowl; the sides will be clean when the dough is ready. If the dough is not elastic enough, mix it for a few more minutes and check again.

Once the dough is ready, add the ham mixture and mix on low speed for another 3 minutes. Work in any ham or spices by hand that are not mixed in.

Form the dough into a ball and put it in a lightly greased bowl. Cover it with lightly greased plastic wrap and let rise in a warm, draft-free place until the dough is 1½ times its original size, about 1½ hours.

Turn out onto a lightly floured work surface and cut into 2 equal pieces. To form each loaf, grab part of the outside edge of the dough between your forefinger and thumb and pull it into the center. Press down firmly and give the dough a quarter turn. Repeat until you have made about three 360° turns (12 quarter turns). Turn the dough over. At this point, it should be round and the outer skin should be sufficiently stretched but not broken. This shaping process is important and will ensure an even form later. Place both balls on a lightly floured baking sheet, cover loosely with lightly greased plastic wrap, and let the dough rise in a warm draft-free place until it has doubled in volume, 2½ to 3 hours.

Position a rack on the lowest rung of the oven and preheat to 475°F. Line a baking sheet with parchment paper, sprinkle with cornmeal, and keep nearby.

After they've doubled in size, transfer the dough balls to the prepared baking sheet. With a single-edge razor blade or a thin sharp knife, make 3 parallel incisions no more than ½-inch deep at a 45° angle. Leave about 1½ inches between each cut.

Use a spray bottle to generously mist the breads with water. Spray the bottom of the oven generously with water and transfer the baking sheet to

the oven. (The steam generated will allow a nice crust to form.) Bake about 45 minutes until the breads are a dark golden brown and sound hollow when tapped. Rotate the pan halfway through the baking. Transfer the loaves to a wire rack to cool.

Sandwich Buns

Makes 10 buns

1 package active dry yeast
1¼ cups lukewarm water (105°–115°F)
3⅓ cups bread flour
1 Tbsp salt
2½ Tbsp sugar
¼ cup milk, at room temperature
2 Tbsp unsalted butter, at room temperature
1 large egg
1 Tbsp heavy cream
Pinch of salt

Stir together the yeast and ¼ cup of the warm water in a small bowl; let stand until creamy, about 5 minutes. Combine the flour, salt, sugar, yeast mixture, remaining water, milk, and butter in the bowl of a mixer fitted with a dough hook. Mix on low speed until the dough comes together, about 3 minutes.

Increase the speed to high and mix for 8 to 10 minutes. (Keep an eye on your mixer; it may shake on the counter as the dough becomes more elastic.)

Stop to check the dough: Wet your fingers and pull off a small piece. Stretch the dough between your fingers. It should be shiny, elastic, and smooth and should not break apart. Also check the inside of the mixer bowl; the sides will be clean when the dough is ready. If the dough is not elastic enough, mix it for a few more minutes and check again.

Transfer the dough to a lightly floured baking sheet, cover with a damp kitchen towel, and let it rest for 30 minutes.

Line two baking sheets with parchment paper. Cut the dough into 10 equal pieces (each weighing about 2½ ounces). On a lightly floured work surface, using the edge of your hand, roll each piece of dough firmly in a circular motion, curling your fingers to create a mold. The dough should pop up into your palm, having formed a tight, smooth skin. Or place each piece of dough in a 3-inch bottomless tart ring. Making sure that the palm of your hand is touching the surface of the dough, move the ring in a circular motion until the dough forms a tight ball. Place the balls on the prepared baking sheets, cover with a damp towel, and let rest for 20 minutes.

With the palm of your hand, smack each piece of dough to form flat discs. Let rise about 3 hours in a warm draft-free area or until the dough has doubled in volume. Whisk together the egg, heavy cream, and salt and very gently brush the top of each bun with the egg wash.

Meanwhile, preheat the oven to 450°F. Put the buns in the oven and bake 15 to 20 minutes until golden brown. Transfer to a rack to cool.

SUGGESTED SANDWICH FILLING

1. Fresh roasted red peppers, anchovy fillets, sliced ricotta salata, arugula, and basil leaves, all sprinkled with extra-virgin olive oil

2. Thin-sliced prosciutto, oven-baked red-onion wheels, chopped fresh sage, and black-truffle shavings

3. Mashed avocado, tomato slices, poached shrimp, coriander, grated lime zest, olive oil, and a dash of Tabasco

Mini Baguettes and Butter Balls

*Makes approximately 12 mini baguettes
or 20 small butter balls*

Cornmeal
2⅔ cups bread flour
1 cup plus 2 Tbsp cold water
2 tsp fine sea salt
½ Tbsp unsalted butter
1 tsp active dry yeast
For butter balls only: 4 Tbsp salted butter,
    cut into 20 cubes

Line a baking sheet with parchment paper and sprinkle with cornmeal. Combine the flour and water in the bowl of a mixer fitted with a dough hook. Mix on low speed until the dough is homogenous, about 3 minutes. Cover the bowl with plastic wrap, and let the dough rest for 15 to 20 minutes.

Add the salt, unsalted butter, and yeast, and mix on low speed for 1 minute to incorporate. Increase the speed to high and beat for 8 to 10 minutes. (Keep an eye on the mixer; it may shake on the counter as the dough becomes more elastic.)

Stop to check the dough: Wet your fingers and pull off a small piece. Stretch the dough between your fingers. It should be shiny, elastic, and smooth and should not break apart. Also check the inside of the bowl; the sides should be clean when the dough is ready. If the dough is not elastic enough, mix it for a few more minutes and check again.

Form the dough into a ball and place it in a lightly greased bowl. Cover with lightly greased plastic wrap and let rise in a warm, draft-free area until the dough is 1½ times its original size, about 1 hour.

Turn out onto a lightly floured work surface, and cut the dough into 12 equal pieces for mini-baguettes or 20 pieces for butter balls. Form each piece into a ball by grabbing a small piece of the outside edge of the dough between your forefinger and thumb and pulling it into the center. Press down firmly and give the dough a quarter turn. Repeat until you have made three 360° turns (12 quarter turns). Turn the dough over. At this point, it should be round and the outer skin should be sufficiently stretched but not broken. This shaping process is important and will ensure an even form. Place the balls on a lightly floured baking sheet, cover loosely with plastic wrap, and let rest for approximately 45 minutes.

FOR MINI BAGUETTES

Gently flatten one ball of dough into a disc with the palm of your hand. Fold the top of the dough over so that it covers two-thirds of itself, then flatten it with the heel of your hand. Give the dough a 180° turn; fold and flatten once again. Then fold the top edge of the dough down into the center and flatten. Fold the bottom edge of the dough into the center and flatten. Roll and stretch the dough using your fingers, applying more pressure at the ends so that they taper. The baguettes should be about 6 inches long. Transfer the baguettes, seam side down, to the prepared baking sheet with cornmeal, leaving at least 1½ inches between each one. Cover loosely with plastic wrap and let rest for 45 minutes.

For Butter Balls

Turn the balls of dough upside down and place a cube of butter on top of each ball. Pinch about ⅛ inch of dough on opposite sides of the ball between your forefingers and thumbs. Stretch the dough to about 1 inch and then fold it into the center overlapping them slightly. Gently press to seal. Give the dough a quarter turn and repeat. Grasp one set of corners on opposite sides and repeat. Repeat with the final set of corners. Invert the balls so they are folded-side down onto a generously floured baking sheet, cover loosely with lightly greased plastic wrap and let rest for 45 minutes.

Meanwhile, position a rack on the lowest rung of the oven and preheat to 475°F.

If making baguettes, use a single-edge razor blade or a thin sharp knife to slash the dough at a 45° angle lengthwise four times; each cut should be about 1½ inches long. If making butter balls, arrange the balls flour side up on the prepared baking sheet with cornmeal, leaving at least 1½ inches between the rolls.

Use a spray bottle to generously mist the breads with water. Very generously spray the bottom of the oven with water and transfer the tray to the oven. The steam generated will allow a nice crust to form. Bake about 20 minutes until the breads are crisp and browned on the outside and sound hollow when tapped on the bottom. Transfer to a wire rack to cool. *(Instead of butter, the small round rolls can be filled with olive tapenade, roasted peppers, tomato confit and/or goat cheese, or other ingredients.)*

Chocolate–Rum Pots de Crème
with Cinnamon Sacristains

Makes 4 servings

FOR THE POTS DE CRÈME
¾ cup milk
⅓ cup dark rum
½ cup sugar
3½ ounces bittersweet chocolate, finely chopped
4 large egg yolks, lightly beaten

FOR THE CINNAMON SACRISTAINS
¼ pound frozen puff pastry, thawed
1 large egg, lightly beaten
Sugar for sprinkling
Ground cinnamon for sprinkling

TO MAKE THE POTS DE CRÈME
Center a rack in the oven and preheat to 350°F.

Bring the milk, rum, sugar, and 2 tablespoons water to a boil in a saucepan. Put the chocolate into a bowl and pour the milk mixture over. Using a rubber spatula, gently stir until the chocolate is melted and smooth. Cool to room temperature.

Very gradually and very gently—you don't want to create air bubbles—stir the chocolate mixture into the egg yolks. Strain through a fine-mesh sieve set over a bowl. Press a single paper towel against the surface of the custard to lift off any foam. *(The custard can be covered and refrigerated overnight.)*

Place five 4-ounce espresso or custard cups evenly spaced in a small roasting pan. Fill each cup almost to the top with the custard mixture. Carefully slide the pan partway into the oven, then, using a pitcher, fill the roasting pan with enough hot water to submerge the espresso cups halfway. Cover the pan with plastic wrap and poke holes in two diagonally opposite corners. Bake the custards about 30 minutes until they are set but still jiggle a little in the center when you gently shake them.

Remove the pan from the oven and let the custards sit in the water bath for 10 minutes. Peel off the plastic wrap, carefully lift the cups out of the water, and cool the custards in the refrigerator. *(The pots de crème can be prepared a day ahead and stored in the refrigerator. When they are cool, cover them with plastic wrap.)*

TO MAKE THE SACRISTAINS
Cut the puff pastry into a rectangle measuring approximately 7-by-6-inches. Place the dough on a parchment- or silpat-lined baking sheet. Brush with the beaten egg and sprinkle with sugar and ground cinnamon to taste. Fold the dough in half and refrigerate for at least 1 hour.

Using a very sharp paring knife or pizza cutter, cut the puff pastry into 7-by-¼-inch strips. Put the strips on a flat surface and using the palms of your hands, swivel your hands in opposite directions to twist each one. Return the strips to the baking sheet and refrigerate for 1 hour.

Center a rack in the oven and preheat to 400°F.

Bake 8 to 10 minutes until golden brown. Transfer the sacristains to a wire rack and let cool.

TO SERVE
The pots de crème are best at room temperature. Remove from the refrigerator and keep them out for about 20 minutes before serving with the sacristains.

It is a good idea to pair the intense flavor of the Chocolate Pots de Crème with a naturally sweet red wine that is low in acidity, like the Late Harvest Zinfandel 1999 produced by Linne Colado. Its decadent dark-fruit aromas add a nice contrast to the custard and bring out the rum.

Chamonix à l'Orange

Makes 12 cakes

FOR THE ORANGE COMPOTE
1 large seedless orange
¾ cup sugar

FOR THE CAKES
½ cup all-purpose flour
½ tsp baking powder
¾ tsp ground ginger
Pinch of ground cloves
Pinch of ground star anise
Pinch of salt
5 Tbsp unsalted butter, at room temperature
¼ cup plus 1 Tbsp sugar
1 Tbsp molasses
Finely grated zest of 1 orange
¾ cup freshly squeezed orange juice reduced to
    3 Tbsp
1 large egg, at room temperature

FOR THE GLAZE
2 cups freshly squeezed orange juice reduced to
    ½ cup (about 3 oranges)
2½ cups confectioners' sugar, sifted

TO MAKE THE ORANGE COMPOTE

Finely grate the zest from half of the orange. Peel the orange and chop the fruit. Bring the orange fruit and sugar to a boil in a small saucepan; cook for 10 minutes. Remove from heat and stir in the orange zest. Let cool. *(This recipe makes more than is needed. The extra compote makes an excellent accompaniment for toast, pancakes, brioche, etc.)*

TO MAKE THE CAKES

Center a rack in the oven and preheat to 375°F.

Coat a standard 12-cup muffin pan with nonstick cooking spray and place on a baking sheet.

Sift together the flour, baking powder, ginger, cloves, star anise, and salt. Cream the butter, sugar, molasses, orange zest, and juice with a mixer until light and fluffy. Add the egg, mixing well. Add the dry ingredients and mix just until combined. Using a spoon or a pastry bag without a tip, fill each muffin cup one-quarter full. Bake about 20 minutes until a skewer inserted into the center comes out clean. Let the cakes cool in the pan on a wire rack for 5 minutes. Invert the cakes onto the wire rack, remove the pan, and let cool completely. Reduce the oven temperature to 200°F.

Slice each cake in half horizontally. Place 1 tablespoon of the orange compote on the bottom half of each cake. Replace the top of each cake and press down slightly to seal. Place the cakes on a wire rack set over a jelly-roll pan.

TO MAKE THE GLAZE

Whisk together the orange juice and confectioners' sugar in a small bowl. The glaze should just be thick enough to coat the back of a spoon. If the glaze is too thick, add more orange juice a little at a time. Using a small ladle, spoon the glaze over each cake until completely covered. Put the cakes into the oven and bake about 15 minutes, or until the glaze sets. Serve warm or at room temperature.

Tokaji from Hungary more often than not has interesting candied-orange aromas in addition to its slightly oxidized flavor, which makes it a nice companion to the Chamonix. Its acidity tames the sweetness of the glaze, and its nuttiness infuses the compote with an interesting flavor. A really nice Tokaji is the "4 Puttonyos" 1995 produced by Disznoko.

Chocolate Bread Pudding

with Dried Fruit

Makes 4 or 5 servings

½ cup finely chopped dried apricots, cherries, or figs

7 ounces bittersweet chocolate, finely chopped

1 cup milk

¼ cup heavy cream

2 large eggs

¼ cup sugar

2 Tbsp unsweetened cocoa powder (preferably Dutch process)

4 large plain or chocolate croissants, cut into ½-inch pieces

Center a rack in the oven and preheat to 350°F.

Butter four 4-ounce ramekins (3-by-1½ inches).

Put the dried fruit into a small saucepan, add enough water to cover, and bring to a boil. Drain.

Put the chocolate into a large bowl set over a pan of simmering water, making certain that the bottom of the bowl does not touch the water. Stir periodically with a rubber spatula until the chocolate has melted and is hot. Remove from heat.

Whisk together the milk, cream, eggs, sugar, and cocoa in a medium bowl. Whisk in the melted chocolate until blended. Add the croissants and dried fruit and stir to combine. Divide the mixture evenly among the prepared ramekins. Place the ramekins into a large roasting pan, filling it with enough hot water to submerge the ramekins halfway. Bake 35 to 40 minutes until the custard is set or a small paring knife inserted into the center of a pudding comes out clean. Serve warm.

Rich in spice, dried-fruit, and nut aromas the Barossa Old Tawny made by Trevor Jones in Australia works wonderfully with the bread pudding, picking up its fruit flavors in particular. And the sweet texture of the finish leaves little to be desired. If it's unavailable, a tawny port could also do the trick.

Phyllo Apple Tart

with Calvados Crème Anglaise

Makes 6 servings

FOR THE CALVADOS CRÈME ANGLAISE
1 cup milk
4 Tbsp sugar
½ vanilla bean, split and scraped
1 large egg yolk
3 Tbsp Calvados

FOR THE TART
3 Tbsp unsalted butter
6 Rome apples, peeled, cored, and each cut into
    6 wedges
1 vanilla bean, split and scraped
2 Tbsp granulated sugar
⅓ cup Calvados
⅓ cup clarified butter
8 sheets fresh phyllo dough or thawed if frozen
½ cup confectioners' sugar
⅓ cup sliced blanched almonds

TO MAKE THE CALVADOS CRÈME ANGLAISE
Combine the milk, 2 tablespoons of the sugar, and the vanilla-bean seeds and pod in a small saucepan and bring to a boil over high heat. Remove from heat, cover, and let infuse for 10 minutes. Strain through a fine-mesh sieve into a clean saucepan and bring back to a boil.

Prepare an ice-water bath in a large bowl. In a small bowl, whisk together the remaining 2 tablespoons sugar, and the egg yolk until light and pale. Gradually pour half of the hot milk over the yolk mixture, whisking constantly. Return to the saucepan. Cook 1 to 2 minutes over medium heat, stirring constantly with a wooden spoon, until the mixture thickens and coats the back of the spoon or until it reaches 185°F on an instant-read thermometer. Strain through a fine-mesh sieve into a medium bowl. Place the bowl in the ice-water bath and let cool completely. Stir in the

Calvados. *(The crème anglaise can be prepared up to 1 day ahead and stored in an airtight container in the refrigerator.)*

TO MAKE THE TART
Warm the butter in a large skillet over medium heat until foamy. Add the apples and vanilla-bean seeds and pod, and cook about 15 minutes, tossing frequently, until the apples are lightly caramelized and nearly cooked through. Add the granulated sugar and cook, stirring, for 2 minutes. Add the Calvados and flambé by standing back and carefully tilting the skillet until the Calvados flames. (Or, if using an electric stove, light using a long match.) When the flame dies out, cover the pan and reduce heat to low. Continue to cook the apples until they are very tender but still hold their shape, about 5 minutes more. Remove from heat and set aside to cool. Discard the vanilla bean.

Center a rack in the oven and preheat to 325°F.

Melt the clarified butter in a small saucepan. Put a buttered 10-inch cake ring on top of a baking sheet lined with parchment paper. Place 1 sheet of phyllo dough on a work surface. (Cover the remaining phyllo with a damp towel.) Brush the phyllo sheet with clarified butter and dust with confectioners' sugar. Loosely crumple the phyllo into the ring so that it covers the bottom without coming up the sides. Sprinkle with 1 tablespoon of the almonds. Repeat with 3 more phyllo sheets.

Mound the apples on top of the phyllo, leaving a 1-inch border. Butter and sugar another sheet of phyllo, crumple it over the apples, and sprinkle with the remaining almonds. Top with another sheet of buttered-and-sugared phyllo. Bake about 10 minutes until lightly browned. (If the tart browns too quickly, cover it loosely with aluminum foil.) Remove the tart from the oven and increase the oven temperature to 400°F.

Butter and sugar another sheet of phyllo and put it on top of the tart, crumpling it gently so it remains airy and light. Bake the tart for 7 minutes, then remove from the oven. Add a final sheet of buttered (not sugared) phyllo, dust the tart evenly with the remaining confectioners' sugar, and bake about 8 minutes more, or until the top layer is golden brown and most of the confectioners' sugar has caramelized. (The sugar can burn quickly, so check often.) Transfer the tart to a wire rack and let cool for 5 minutes.

To Serve

Carefully lift off the baking ring and transfer the tart to a tray. Serve warm or at room temperature with the crème anglaise.

The distinct flavors in this simple dessert call for a great Coteaux du Layon "l'Anclaie" Château Pierre-Bise 2001 from the Loire Valley made from Chenin Blanc, with apple and honey aromas. And because the wine is drier than it seems, it brings a touch of lightness to the whole experience.

Chocolate-Ginger Pound Cake

Makes 3 loaves

2 cups all-purpose flour
1 cup unsweetened cocoa powder (preferably Dutch process)
1 tsp salt
½ tsp baking powder
1 cup buttermilk, at room temperature
¼ cup espresso or strong brewed coffee
1 cup (2 sticks) unsalted butter, at room temperature
3 cups granulated sugar
1 vanilla bean, split and scraped
5 large eggs, at room temperature
¾ cup chopped candied ginger
Confectioners' sugar for dusting
Vanilla ice cream for serving

Center a rack in the oven and preheat to 325°F.

Coat three 8½-by-3½-by-2½-inch loaf pans with nonstick cooking spray. Place on a baking sheet.

Sift together the flour, cocoa, salt, and baking powder. Stir together the buttermilk, espresso, and ¼-cup room-temperature water in a liquid measure. Cream the butter, sugar, and vanilla-bean seeds on medium speed with an electric mixer until light and fluffy. Add the eggs, one at a time, mixing well after each addition. On low speed, add the dry ingredients, alternately with the buttermilk mixture, in three batches, ending with the liquid. Stir in the ginger just until combined.

Divide the batter among the prepared loaf pans, smoothing each surface with a rubber spatula. Bake about 70 minutes, until a small paring knife inserted into the center comes out with a few moist crumbs clinging. Rotate the pans halfway through baking.

Let the cakes cool in the pans on a wire rack for 10 minutes. Invert the cakes onto the wire rack, remove the pans, reinvert, and cool completely. Dust the cakes with confectioners' sugar and serve with vanilla ice cream.

The last thing one wants to add to this chocolate-lover's pound cake is more richness. So a light, sparkling dessert wine should be served. The delicate strawberry aromas of the Bugey Cerdon wine made by Renardat-Fache will freshen this dessert, yet it has enough structure to stand up to it, too.

Pineapple and Coconut Givré

Makes 10 servings

FOR THE GIVRÉ
1 very ripe pineapple
One 15-ounce can Coco Lopez
¼ cup dark rum
Freshly squeezed juice of ½ lime

FOR THE DECORATION
2 cups sugar
¼ cup light corn syrup

TO MAKE THE GIVRÉ
Trim the base of the pineapple so that it sits flat. Slice off the top 2 inches of the pineapple, keeping the leaves attached. Carefully cut the crown of leaves out of the fruit cap; discard the cap. Using a small knife and a spoon, scoop out the pineapple pulp, catching all the fruit and juice you can into a bowl; take care not to pierce the shell. Holding the pineapple upside down, scrape the inside to re-move any remaining pulp. Rinse the shell under cold running water. Pat dry, wrap in plastic wrap, and freeze for at least 2 hours or overnight.

Put the fruit and juice into a blender; process until smooth. Strain the juice through a fine-mesh sieve (there will be about 4 cups); discard the pulp.

Stir together the pineapple juice, Coco Lopez, rum, and lime juice. Refrigerate overnight.

The givré's pineapple and coconut flavors and the threads of caramel demand a sweeter, traditional Sauternes-like wine made from late-harvest Sauvignon and Sémillon grapes. Even a non-French version like Fattoria Le Pupille "Sol Alto" 2000 produced in Maremma (Tuscany) should be a crowd pleaser without stealing the show.

Freeze the cold pineapple mixture in an ice-cream maker following the manufacturer's directions. Working quickly, unwrap the frozen pineapple, fill it just to the top with the sorbet and return it to the freezer along with the unused sorbet.

TO MAKE THE DECORATION
Line a work surface and 3 baking sheets with parchment paper; lightly coat each with vegetable spray. Prepare an ice-water bath in a large bowl.

Bring the sugar and ½ cup water to a boil in a heavy, medium saucepan. Stir until the sugar dis-solves, washing down any crystals from the sides of the pan with a wet brush. Bring the syrup to a boil—don't stir—and cook until light golden brown. Remove the pan from the heat and immerse the bottom in the ice water for 30 seconds. Set the pan down on a heatproof surface and let the caramel rest until it forms a thin thread when drizzled, about 8 minutes.

Lightly coat the handles of two wooden spoons with vegetable spray. Set four soup cans on the parchment-paper-lined surface. Rest one end of each spoon on a separate soup can; the spoons should be parallel to each other and about 15 inches apart. Intertwine the tines of two forks and hold them in one hand. Dip the tines into the warm caramel, letting the excess drip back into the pot. Rapidly wave the tines back and forth over the middle portion of the two spoons to cre-ate a series of sugar threads. Repeat a couple of times, until you have a light, airy layer of spun sugar. If the caramel in the pot hardens, warm it over low heat. Gently place the spun-sugar layer on a prepared baking sheet. Continue spinning sugar layers until you have enough to form a base for the pineapple givré—it should be as light and lovely as a golden cloud.

To Serve
Place the givré-filled pineapple on a large platter. Cover it with scoops of the unused sorbet and top with the reserved pineapple crown. Make a spun-sugar base for the pineapple (see photo).

Chocolate Cakes

with Nut Caramel

Makes 6 servings

FOR THE CARAMEL
1¼ cups light corn syrup
1 cup sugar
9 Tbsp salted butter, cut into small pieces
½ cup heavy cream
¾ cup skinned hazelnuts
⅔ cup skinned whole almonds

FOR THE CAKES
5 ounces semisweet or bittersweet chocolate, coarsely chopped
3 Tbsp unsalted butter
3 Tbsp heavy cream
2 large eggs
3 Tbsp sugar
2 Tbsp all-purpose flour
1 ounce milk chocolate, coarsely chopped

TO MAKE THE CARAMEL
Line two 9-by-5-by-3-inch metal loaf pans with plastic wrap, allowing it to extend over the sides by 2 inches.

Combine the corn syrup and sugar in a medium saucepan. Bring to a boil over high heat. Cook, stirring occasionally, until the caramel has turned a dark-amber color; deglaze with the butter, and heavy cream. Continue to cook the caramel, stirring, until it reaches 239°F on a candy thermometer. Immediately add the nuts and divide evenly between the two prepared pans. Let cool for 3 hours.

Cut the caramel into ½-inch squares. If not using right away, store in an airtight container in the refrigerator for up to 1 month. *(This recipe makes more caramel than needed for the chocolate cakes.)*

TO MAKE THE CAKES
Center a rack in the oven and preheat to 350°F.

Coat six standard muffin cups with nonstick cooking spray and place on a baking sheet.

Place the chocolate, butter, and cream in a medium bowl over a pan of simmering water, making certain that the bottom of the bowl does not touch the water. Stir occasionally until the chocolate melts and the mixture is smooth. Remove from heat. Whisk together the eggs, sugar, and flour in a large bowl. Fold the chocolate-butter mixture into the egg mixture until they are well blended but not overmixed.

Fill each muffin cup one-third full with the batter. Place 1 caramel square in the center of each cup, and sprinkle the milk chocolate over. Spoon in the remaining batter, covering the caramel and chocolate completely.

Bake 8 to 9 minutes, until the top of the cake is dry and shiny, rotating the pan halfway through the baking. Remove the pan from the oven and let cool on a wire rack for 5 minutes. Carefully remove the cakes from the pan and serve immediately. *(To serve later, reheat the cakes in a 350°F oven for 2 to 3 minutes.)*

The alliance among the sweet, bitter, and dark-berry flavors in this wonderful Banyuls 1985 from Dr. Parcé—France's answer to Port—really highlights the richness of these chocolate and caramel cakes. Still, the tannic kick and noticeable acidity prevent the pairing from being too sweet and heavy.

Trio of Chocolate Ice Creams

Each recipe makes about 1½ quarts of ice cream

FOR THE SPICED MILK-CHOCOLATE ICE CREAM
4 cups milk
⅓ cup heavy cream
½ cup sugar
6½ Tbsp light corn syrup
2 tsp pink peppercorns, crushed
½ tsp coriander seeds, crushed
2 pinches of saffron threads
1 allspice berry
1 cardamom pod, crushed
⅛ tsp yellow mustard seeds
8 large egg yolks
11 ounces milk chocolate, finely chopped
1 tsp apricot-flavored liqueur

Combine the milk, cream, 2 tablespoons of the sugar, the corn syrup, peppercorns, coriander, saffron, allspice, cardamom, and mustard seeds in a medium saucepan and bring to a boil over high heat. Remove from heat, cover, and infuse for 10 minutes. Strain through a fine-mesh sieve into a clean saucepan and bring back to a boil.

Prepare an ice-water bath in a large bowl. Whisk together the remaining 6 tablespoons sugar and the egg yolks in a medium bowl until light and pale. Gradually pour half of the hot-milk mixture over the yolks while whisking constantly. Pour the mixture back into the saucepan. Cook 1 to 2 minutes over medium heat, stirring constantly with a wooden spoon, until the mixture thickens and coats the back of the spoon or reaches 185°F on an instant-read thermometer. Strain through a fine-mesh sieve into a large bowl. Add the milk chocolate and stir until the chocolate has melted and the mixture is smooth. Place the bowl in the ice-water bath and cool completely. Stir in the apricot liqueur.

Freeze the custard in an ice-cream maker according to the manufacturer's instructions. Transfer to a covered container and freeze for at least 1 hour before serving.

FOR THE WHITE-CHOCOLATE PASSION-FRUIT ICE CREAM
4 cups milk
⅔ cup heavy cream
¾ cup sugar
4½ Tbsp light corn syrup
7 large egg yolks
7 ounces white chocolate, finely chopped
⅔ cup passion-fruit puree or juice
Finely grated zest of 4 limes
Freshly squeezed juice of 2 limes

Combine the milk, cream, ¼ cup of the sugar, and corn syrup in a medium saucepan and bring to a boil over high heat.

Prepare an ice-water bath in a large bowl. Whisk together the remaining ½ cup sugar and the egg yolks in a medium bowl until light and pale. Gradually pour half of the hot-milk mixture over the yolks while whisking constantly. Pour the mixture back into the saucepan. Cook 2 to 3 minutes over medium heat, stirring constantly with a wooden spoon, until the mixture thickens and coats the back of the spoon or reaches 185°F on an instant-read thermometer. Strain through a fine-mesh sieve into a large bowl. Add the chocolate, the juice, and the lime zest and stir until the chocolate has melted and the mixture is smooth. Place the bowl in the ice-water bath and cool completely.

Freeze the custard in an ice-cream maker according to the manufacturer's instructions. Transfer to a covered container and freeze for at least 1 hour before serving.

For the Rosemary-Orange Chocolate Ice Cream

4 cups milk
¾ cup heavy cream
⅔ cup sugar
2 Tbsp light corn syrup
2 sprigs rosemary
10 large egg yolks
6 ounces bittersweet chocolate, finely chopped
Finely grated zest of 1 orange
Freshly squeezed juice of 1 orange

Combine the milk, cream, ⅓ cup of the sugar, corn syrup, and the rosemary in a medium saucepan and bring to a boil over high heat. Remove from heat, cover, and infuse for 15 minutes. Strain through a fine-mesh sieve into a clean saucepan and return to a boil.

Prepare an ice-water bath in a large bowl. Whisk together the remaining ⅓ cup sugar and the egg yolks in a medium bowl until light and pale. Gradually pour half of the hot-milk mixture over the yolks while whisking constantly. Pour the mixture back into the saucepan. Cook 1 to 2 minutes over medium heat, stirring constantly with a wooden spoon, until the mixture thickens and coats the back of the spoon or reaches 185°F on an instant-read thermometer. Strain through a fine-mesh sieve into a large bowl. Add the chocolate, the juice, and the orange zest and stir until the chocolate has melted and the mixture is smooth. Place the bowl in the ice-water bath and cool completely.

Freeze the custard in an ice-cream maker according to the manufacturer's instructions. Transfer to a covered container and freeze for at least 1 hour before serving.

Two words: Rosé champagne. Taittinger makes a wonderful version. Its dry character and fine bubbles give a steely backbone to the richness of the ice creams.

Passion–Fruit Soufflés

with Caramelized Pear-Passion Sauce

Makes 4 servings

FOR THE SAUCE

1 Tbsp unsalted butter
½ cup sugar
2 ripe pears, peeled, cored, and cut into small
   pieces
¼ cup passion-fruit puree

FOR THE SOUFFLÉS

4 large egg yolks, at room temperature
¼ cup passion-fruit puree
¾ cup egg whites (about 4 large eggs),
   at room temperature
¼ cup plus 1 Tbsp sugar
Confectioners' sugar, for dusting

TO MAKE THE SAUCE

Melt the butter in a large skillet over medium-high heat. Add the sugar, a few tablespoons at a time, stirring, until it melts. Cook until the syrup turns a light golden brown.

Add the pear and continue to cook for 10 minutes, stirring, until the pears are tender and nicely caramelized. Stir in the passion-fruit puree and heat for a minute or two. Remove from the heat and keep warm while preparing the soufflés.

A 1998 Monbazillac from Château Tirecul La Gravière, a luscious late-harvest blend of Sauvignon Blanc and sweet Sémillon grapes will coax out the passion fruit perfectly.

TO MAKE THE SOUFFLÉS

Center a rack in the oven and preheat to 375°F.

Generously butter the inside and rims of four 6-ounce soufflé dishes. Dust the insides and rims with sugar, making certain that they are thoroughly coated. Tap out the excess sugar and put the dishes on a baking sheet.

Whisk together the egg yolks and passion-fruit puree in a large bowl until well blended; set aside.

Put the egg whites in the bowl of a mixer fitted with a whisk attachment. Beat on medium-low speed just until foamy. Increase the speed to medium-high and gradually add the sugar, beating until the whites form glossy medium-stiff peaks. Using a large rubber spatula and a light touch, fold the meringue into the yolk mixture in three batches until well incorporated but not overmixed.

Fit a pastry bag with a large plain round tip and fill with the soufflé mixture. Pipe (or if you prefer spoon) the mixture into the dishes up to their rims. Run your thumb along the outside edge to remove any excess butter and sugar. Bake the soufflés 15 to 20 minutes, until puffed and lightly golden. If you touch the tops of the soufflés, they should be firm with centers that are still a bit jiggly.

Meanwhile, transfer the sauce to a warm sauceboat; keep warm.

When the soufflés are done, carefully remove the baking sheet from the oven. Dust the tops of the soufflés with confectioners' sugar and serve immediately with the pear-passion sauce.

Frozen Strawberry Soufflés

Makes 6 servings

4½ pints ripe strawberries, hulled
1 cup sugar
5 large egg whites
½ tsp freshly squeezed lemon juice
2 cups heavy cream

Cut ½ pint of strawberries into thin slices. Cut each slice in half.

Place six 6-ounce soufflé dishes (3½-by-2 inches) on a baking sheet. Cut twelve 22-by-4-inch strips of parchment paper or wax paper. Wrap a strip tightly around the outside of each ramekin (it should reach around twice) to form a paper collar and secure with a paper clip. Line the strawberry slices, upright, along the rim of each dish, making sure they are pressed firmly to the side of the paper collar.

Put the remaining 4 pints of strawberries into a blender or food processor and puree until smooth. Strain though a fine-mesh sieve, measure out 2 cups of puree and reserve the rest.

Place ¾ cup of the sugar and ¼ cup water in a medium saucepan and bring to a boil. Cook until the mixture reaches 250°F on a candy thermometer, while loosening any crystals that form on the side of the saucepan with a pastry brush dipped in cold water.

Meanwhile, put the egg whites in the bowl of a mixer fitted with a whisk attachment. Whip on low speed for 2 minutes, then increase the speed to medium. Add the lemon juice and keep whipping until the whites hold soft peaks. Add the remaining ¼ cup sugar and whip until firm peaks form.

Using a whisk, whip the cream in a bowl until it barely holds soft peaks. Do not overwhip. Refrigerate.

When the syrup reaches 250°F, pour it into the egg whites in a fine stream against the side of the bowl while mixing on low speed. When all of the syrup has been added, increase the speed to high and whip until the meringue increases significantly in volume, turns glossy, and is cool to the touch.

Gently fold 1 cup of the strawberry puree into the whipped cream and the remaining cup of puree into the egg-white mixture. Fold the egg-white mixture into the strawberry whipped cream. Fill each dish with an equal amount of batter (it will rise above the rims). Carefully smooth the tops with the back of a spoon. Freeze overnight.

To Serve
Remove the soufflés from the freezer and carefully remove the paper collars. Let sit at room temperature for about 20 minutes. Serve with the reserved strawberry puree.

What better than a Daniel invention: a strawberry-infused Berrini will keep this summery soufflé sparkling fresh.

Chocolate Mousse

2¼ cups heavy cream
8 ounces bittersweet chocolate, finely chopped
⅔ cup plus ½ cup sugar
6 large eggs, separated
3 large eggs
Chocolate shavings for serving
Whipped cream for serving

In the bowl of a mixer fitted with a whisk attachment, whip the cream until it barely holds soft peaks. Do not overwhip. Set aside.

Put the chocolate into a large bowl set over a pan of simmering water, making certain that the bottom of the bowl does not touch the water. Stir occasionally with a rubber spatula until the chocolate has melted and is hot. Remove from heat.

Combine the ⅔ cup sugar and ¼ cup water in a small, heavy saucepan; bring to a boil without stirring. Cover and boil until the sugar has completely dissolved. Uncover and keep boiling until the mixture reaches the soft-ball stage, 240°F, on a candy thermometer.

Meanwhile, beat the egg yolks and whole eggs in the bowl of a mixer fitted with the whisk attachment until thick and pale. When the syrup is at 240°F, pour it into the eggs in a fine stream, beating at high speed until the mixture is cool, 8 to 10 minutes. Transfer to another bowl and set aside. Wash the mixer bowl and whisk.

Put the egg whites into the clean mixer bowl, again fitted with the whisk attachment. Beat while gently adding the remaining ½ cup sugar. After all the sugar has been added, place the bowl over a pot of barely simmering water, making certain that the bottom of the bowl does not touch the water. Stir until the mixture is hot. Reattach the bowl to the mixer and whip with the whisk, until the meringue holds tall, stiff, glossy peaks.

Fold a third of the yolk mixture into the meringue. Working very quickly, fold the whipped cream into the hot melted chocolate (if the chocolate is not hot, rewarm over simmering water or in the microwave). Fold in the rest of the yolk mixture and then the meringue until just blended. Spoon the mousse into a large serving bowl and refrigerate until chilled, about 2 hours.

To Serve
Serve family-style with chocolate shavings and whipped cream alongside in separate bowls.

This mousse lends itself well to a fine glass of sparkling wine. The dry "Le Rêve" made by Domaine Carneros in California, with its nutty overtones, is quite elegant. And it keeps the dessert light by cutting through the richness without interfering with the pure bittersweet chocolate flavors.

Chocolate and Pistachio Crêpes Suzette

Makes 6 to 8 servings

1 large orange: ½ zest removed with a vegetable peeler and julienned; ½ zest finely grated
1⅓ cups plus 3 Tbsp sugar
6½ Tbsp unsalted butter
¾ cup all-purpose flour, sifted
½ cup hazelnut flour, sifted
¼ cup unsweetened cocoa powder (preferably Dutch process), sifted
⅛ tsp plus a pinch of salt
3 large eggs
1 Tbsp dark rum
2 cups milk
4 ounces milk chocolate, coarsely chopped
½ cup pistachios, coarsely chopped
1¼ cups freshly squeezed orange juice
⅔ cup heavy cream
Confectioners' sugar, for dusting

Bring a small saucepan of cold water and the julienned orange zest to a boil. Drain. Return the orange zest to the saucepan. Add 1 cup of water and ⅓ cup sugar and bring to a boil. Lower the heat and simmer for 30 minutes. Cool the zest in the syrup. *(The orange zest can be prepared a day ahead and refrigerated in the sugar syrup in a covered container.)*

Melt 1½ tablespoons of the butter. Whisk together the all-purpose flour, hazelnut flour, cocoa, 3 tablespoons of the sugar, ⅛ teaspoon salt, and the eggs just until combined. Whisk in the melted butter, followed by the rum, grated orange zest, and milk, just until each ingredient is incorporated. For convenience, pour the batter into a pitcher with a spout. Cover the pitcher with plastic wrap and refrigerate for at least 1 hour, or preferably overnight.

When ready to make the crêpes, set a large plate or a small baking sheet close to the stove and line with a piece of plastic wrap. Heat a nonstick 8-inch crêpe pan over medium-high heat. While the pan is warming, melt 1 tablespoon of the butter in another pan. Stir the crêpe batter to bring it together again.

Swirl a few drops of the melted butter over the bottom of the hot crêpe pan. Lift the pan off the heat and pour in about 2 tablespoons of batter, tilting the pan and swirling the batter so that it covers the bottom of the pan in a very thin even layer. Return the pan to the heat and cook the crêpe until it starts to bubble on top. Run a blunt knife or spatula around the edge of the crêpe, then lift it up with your fingers and flip it over. Cook the other side for only about 20 seconds. Transfer to the lined plate and continue making crêpes, dotting the pan with melted butter and gently stirring the batter between crêpes, until you've used all the batter. You should have about 8 crêpes. As the crêpes are made, stack them on the plate.

When the crêpes are cool, put an equal amount of the chocolate and pistachios in the center of each one. Fold the crêpes in half and then in half again, to form a wedge. *(They can be covered with plastic wrap and refrigerated up to 1 day.)*

Warm a medium saucepan over medium-low heat. Sprinkle the remaining cup of sugar into the saucepan a little at a time, and as the sugar melts, add more while stirring. When the caramel has turned a dark-amber color, add the orange juice, heavy cream and a pinch of salt. Continue to cook, stirring, until the caramel has dissolved. Bring to a boil and cook for 4 minutes.

A medium-bodied 10-year-old tawny Port like those produced by Taylor or Fonseca will draw the chocolate and nut flavors from the crêpes while offering a counterpoint to the slightly bitter orange zests.

Warm the remaining 2 tablespoons of butter in a large nonstick skillet over medium heat. Add ½ cup of the caramel to the pan. Add half of the crêpes and rewarm, for about 2 minutes on each side. Repeat with the remaining crêpes and caramel. Transfer each crêpe to a warm dinner plate, dust with confectioners' sugar and drizzle with some of the warm sauce. Serve immediately.

Kiwi Pâtes de Fruits

Makes about 64 jellies

2½ cups kiwi puree (approximately 12 peeled kiwis)
1¾ cups plus ⅓ cup sugar
1 cup powdered pectin
Sugar for coating

Line an 8-inch square baking pan with plastic wrap, allowing it to extend over the sides and smoothing it out with your fingers so that there are no wrinkles. Place on a flat surface.

Bring the kiwi puree and the 1¾ cups sugar to a rolling boil in a medium saucepan. Whisk together the pectin and the remaining ⅓ cup sugar in a small bowl and add to the puree in a fine stream, whisking constantly. Return the mixture to a full boil and cook for 2 minutes over high heat, whisking constantly. Pour into the prepared pan. Allow the mixture to set completely at room temperature (do not move the pan), 30 minutes to 1 hour.

Use the plastic wrap to lift the jellies from the pan onto a cutting board. Using a thin sharp knife, cut the jellies into 1-inch squares. *(The jellies can be stored in an airtight container topped with a sheet of parchment paper or waxed paper at room temperature for up to 10 days.)* Roll in sugar before serving.

Other flavored fruit jellies—such as raspberry and apricot—can be made by adjusting the amount of sugar, depending on the acidity of the fruit.

The scent of aged fruits pervades the dry, powerful Hine Rare & Delicate Cognac, an excellent foil for the fruit jellies.

Rice Pudding Parfaits
with Raspberries and Green-Tea Cream

Makes 6 servings

FOR THE SAUCE
1 cup raspberries
2 Tbsp sugar

FOR THE RICE PUDDING
1¼ cups water
⅓ cup Arborio rice
Pinch of salt
1⅓ cups milk
½ cup heavy cream
⅓ cup plus 1 Tbsp sugar
One 12-ounce can lychees, drained, or 1 pound
    fresh lychees, peeled and pitted

FOR THE GREEN-TEA CREAM
1¾ cups heavy cream
⅓ cup sugar
¼ cup loosely packed oolong tea leaves
½ tsp unflavored gelatin
½ tsp matcha (powdered Japanese green tea)

TO MAKE THE SAUCE
Combine the raspberries and sugar in a small saucepan and bring to a boil over medium-high heat. Strain through a fine-mesh sieve into a bowl. Divide the sauce among six 8-ounce martini glasses. Refrigerate.

TO MAKE THE RICE PUDDING
Line an 8-inch-square baking pan with a piece of plastic wrap.

Combine the water, rice, and salt in a medium saucepan and bring to a boil. Reduce the heat and simmer until the rice has absorbed almost all the water. Meanwhile, stir together the milk, ¼ cup of the heavy cream, and sugar in a small saucepan and warm over medium heat.

Add ½ cup of the warm-milk mixture to the rice and cook, stirring constantly with a wooden spoon, until the rice has absorbed almost all the milk. Repeat, adding ½ cup of the milk mixture at a time to the rice. (Work just as if you were making a risotto.) When all the milk has been added, continue to cook, stirring constantly, until the rice is creamy, not soupy. Remove from heat.

Immediately spread the rice pudding in a thin layer in the prepared pan. Top with another piece of plastic wrap and press the wrap against the pudding to create an airtight seal. Let cool to room temperature.

Whisk the remaining ¼ cup heavy cream to medium peaks in a small bowl. Gently combine the cream into the cooled rice pudding. Spoon half of the rice pudding over the raspberry sauce. Place 4 or 5 lychees on top of the pudding in each glass. Divide the remaining rice pudding among the glasses, making sure the lychees are covered. Refrigerate.

TO MAKE THE GREEN-TEA CREAM
Prepare an ice-water bath in a large bowl. Bring the heavy cream and sugar to a boil in a small saucepan. Add the tea leaves; cover and let infuse for 10 minutes. Strain through a fine-mesh sieve into a bowl, making sure to push down on the leaves to extract all the liquid. Pour 1 cup of the infused cream into a small bowl and set it in the ice water. Stir until cool. Using a whisk, whip the cream to stiff peaks. Refrigerate.

Sprinkle the gelatin over 1 tablespoon cold water in a cup; let soften for 5 minutes.

Combine the remaining infused cream and the green-tea powder in a small saucepan and bring to a boil over high heat. Add the gelatin and stir to dissolve. Transfer to a small bowl and set it in the ice

water. Stir until cool. Fold in the whipped cream. Immediately spoon over the rice pudding, dividing it evenly. Refrigerate for 1 hour before serving.

This complex and delicious recipe may be inspired by Asia, but it pairs beautifully with Cerdon du Bugey, a sweet light-red sparkling wine from Daniel's native region of Lyons. Its upfront berry flavors play off the raspberries and the discreet tannins are a delight with the green-tea cream.

Spiced Chocolate Soup
with Caramel Whipped Cream

Makes 4 servings

8 Tbsp sugar
1 Tbsp unsalted butter
Pinch of salt
1½ cups heavy cream
7 ounces semisweet or bittersweet chocolate,
　finely chopped
2½ cups milk
1 Tbsp Szechuan peppercorns, crushed

Warm a small saucepan over medium-low heat. Sprinkle 5 tablespoons of the sugar into the pan, a little at a time, adding more as it melts. When the caramel has turned a deep golden brown, add the butter, salt, and 1 cup of the heavy cream; bring to a boil, stirring to dissolve the caramel. Refrigerate for at least 6 hours, or preferably overnight.

Transfer the cooled cream into the bowl of a mixer fitted with a whisk attachment and whip until medium peaks form. Refrigerate.

Put the chocolate in a medium bowl. Bring the milk and the remaining 3 tablespoons of sugar to a boil in a medium saucepan. Add the peppercorns and remove from the heat. Cover and let infuse for 15 minutes. Strain the milk through a fine-mesh sieve into a saucepan and bring to a boil. Pour the liquid over the chocolate and stir until the chocolate has melted and the mixture is smooth. Strain through a fine-mesh sieve into a bowl.

To Serve
Ladle the soup into warm bowls and serve topped with a dollop of the caramel whipped cream.

This delectable winter dessert and a Calvados will warm chilly bones. The brandy's richness will underscore the chocolate while its upfront apple aromas will accentuate the soup's spicy overtones. The small house of Camut in Normandy makes an outstanding version.

Cherry Clafoutis

Makes 8 servings

½ cup hazelnuts, skinned and toasted
1 Tbsp all-purpose flour
⅓ cup plus 1 Tbsp sugar
Pinch of salt
2 large eggs
3 large egg yolks
⅔ cup heavy cream
1 cup dark sweet cherries, stemmed and pitted
1½ Tbsp brandy or cognac (optional)
⅓ cup sliced almonds
Confectioners' sugar for dusting

Put the hazelnuts and flour into a food processor and pulse until the nuts are finely ground.

Whisk together the hazelnut mixture, sugar, and salt in a mixing bowl. Add the eggs, then mix in the yolks; add the heavy cream and mix until a smooth batter forms (break up any lumps that form). Transfer the batter to a covered container and refrigerate overnight.

Marinate the cherries in the brandy or cognac, if using, in the refrigerator overnight.

Center a rack in the oven and preheat to 350°F.

Butter an 8-inch pie plate and place on a baking sheet.

Gently whisk the clafoutis batter until smooth and blended. Pour ¾ cup of the batter into the prepared pie plate. Arrange the cherries over the batter in a single layer. Pour the remaining batter over the cherries. Sprinkle the almonds on top.

Bake 30 to 40 minutes, until the clafoutis is puffed and golden brown and a knife inserted into the center comes out clean. Dust the clafoutis with confectioners' sugar and serve warm.

The cherries call for a sweet wine, such as a late-harvest Canadian Riesling by Cave Spring or an Italian Prosecco from the Friuli-Venezia-Giulia region.

Squash Panna Cotta
with Cranberry Compote and Walnut Tuiles

FOR THE PANNA COTTA

3 cups milk

Four ¼-inch-thick slices peeled ginger

1 vanilla bean, split and scraped

1 (3 inches) cinnamon stick

1 strip orange zest, removed with a vegetable peeler

2 points star anise

¼ tsp salt

1¾ pounds kabocha or butternut squash, peeled, seeded and cut into 1-inch chunks

6 Tbsp sugar

1¼ to 2 cups heavy cream

1 packet unflavored gelatin

FOR THE CRANBERRY COMPOTE

3 cups fresh or frozen cranberries

¾ cup sugar

¾ cup water

Two ¼-inch-thick slices peeled ginger

½ vanilla bean, split and scraped

½ (3 inches) cinnamon stick

Pinch of salt

FOR THE WALNUT TUILES

3 Tbsp unsalted butter, melted and cooled

1 Tbsp light corn syrup

¼ cup sugar

½ cup finely chopped walnuts

To Make the Panna Cotta

Combine the milk, ginger, vanilla-bean pod and seed, cinnamon, orange zest, star anise, and salt in a medium saucepan and bring to a simmer. Remove from heat, cover, and let infuse for 20 minutes.

Strain the milk through a fine-mesh sieve set over a bowl. Return to the same saucepan and add the squash. Bring to a boil, reduce the heat to a simmer and poach until the squash is very tender, about 20 minutes. Add the sugar, stir until dissolved, and remove from heat.

Transfer the squash mixture to a blender or food processor and puree until smooth. Strain through a fine-mesh sieve into a 4-cup liquid measure; discard the solids. Add enough cream to equal 3½ cups; stir to combine.

Sprinkle the gelatin over 2 tablespoons water in a small saucepan; let stand 5 minutes to soften. Add ½ cup of the squash puree to the gelatin. Warm over low heat, stirring until the gelatin dissolves. Stir into the remaining squash mixture.

Divide the panna-cotta mixture among eight 4-ounce ramekins. Refrigerate overnight.

To Make the Cranberry Compote

Combine all the ingredients in a small saucepan; cook 10 to 15 minutes over medium heat, stirring, until the cranberries start to lose their shape and most of the liquid has evaporated.

Remove from heat. Scrape the compote onto a plate and press a piece of plastic wrap against the surface of the compote. Refrigerate for at least 1 hour. Before serving, discard the ginger, vanilla-bean pod, and cinnamon stick. Serve chilled or at room temperature.

To Make the Walnut Tuiles

Whisk together the butter, corn syrup, sugar, and walnuts in a small bowl. Cover with plastic wrap, pressing the plastic directly against the surface of the batter. Refrigerate for at least 2 hours or overnight.

Center a rack in the oven and preheat to 350°F.

For each tuile, drop ½ teaspoon of the batter onto a non-stick baking sheet, leaving 2 inches between each drop of batter. Press the batter lightly with your thumb until each drop is about 1 inch in diameter. Bake for 8 to 10 minutes until the tuiles are thin, lacy, and golden brown. Take them out of the oven, wait 1 minute, and then using a plastic spatula, remove the tuiles from the baking sheet; cool on a flat counter. Store in an airtight container in a cool, dry environment.

To Serve

To unmold, run the tip of a small knife around the edges of the panna cottas. Dip the ramekin halfway into a bowl of hot water for 5 to 10 seconds. Dry the bottom and invert onto a dessert plate. Tap lightly to release. Garnish with a spoonful of cranberry compote and a walnut tuile.

A powerful Italian Vin Santo will surely liven up this wonderful panna cotta. The wine's sweet spices and aromas will call attention to the star anise and ginger in the dessert, and its lush structure will counterbalance the acidity of the cranberry compote.

Trio of Cupcakes

FOR THE CHOCOLATE-COFFEE CUPCAKES WITH MOCHA GANACHE AND MASCARPONE CREAM
(makes 30 cupcakes)

½ cup plus 2 Tbsp milk
6 Tbsp unsweetened cocoa powder
   (preferably Dutch Process)
¼ cup instant-coffee powder
1½ cups cake flour
½ tsp baking soda
¼ tsp salt
12 Tbsp (1½ sticks) unsalted butter,
   at room temperature
1 cup plus 2 Tbsp granulated sugar
½ tsp vanilla extract
3 large eggs
3 cups heavy cream
⅓ cup coffee beans, crushed
8 ounces milk chocolate, finely chopped
2 cups mascarpone cheese
¼ cup confectioners' sugar, sifted

TO MAKE THE CHOCOLATE-COFFEE CUPCAKES
Preheat the oven to 350°F. Line 30 standard muffin cups with paper liners.

Combine the milk, cocoa, coffee and ¼ cup water in a small saucepan and bring to a boil, constantly whisking, until the cocoa and coffee have dissolved. Let cool and pour into a liquid measure.

Sift together the flour, baking soda, and salt. In the bowl of a mixer, cream the butter, sugar and vanilla on medium speed until light and fluffy. Add the eggs, one at a time, mixing well after each addition. With the mixer on low speed, add the dry ingredients alternately with the milk mixture in three batches, ending with the liquid. Fill each muffin cup halfway with the batter. Bake 18 to 20 minutes until a toothpick inserted into the center comes out clean. Remove the cupcakes from the pan and let cool completely on a wire rack.

TO MAKE THE MOCHA GANACHE AND MASCARPONE CREAM
Combine 1 cup of the heavy cream and coffee beans in a small saucepan and bring to a boil over high heat. Remove from the heat, cover, and let infuse for 10 minutes. Strain through a fine-mesh sieve into a clean saucepan and bring back to a boil. Put the chocolate in a medium bowl and pour the hot cream over it, stirring slowly, until the ganache is smooth. Spoon enough ganache over each cupcake to fill the liners to the rim.

Using a whisk or in the bowl of a mixer fitted with a whisk attachment, whip the remaining 2 cups of heavy cream to stiff peaks. Add the mascarpone and confectioners' sugar and whisk until smooth. Spoon the mascarpone cream into a pastry bag fitted with a medium round tip and pipe the cream on top of the ganache in a circle.

For the Lemon Cupcakes with Mixed Berries and Ricotta Cream

(makes about 18 cupcakes)

1½ cups cake flour
1 tsp baking powder
½ tsp salt
8 Tbsp (1 stick) unsalted butter, at room
    temperature
1 cup granulated sugar
1½ tsp vanilla extract
Finely grated zest of 2 lemons
3 large eggs, at room temperature
¾ cup milk
1 cup heavy cream
1½ cups ricotta cheese
3 Tbsp confectioners' sugar
1 cup mixed berries, such as strawberries,
    raspberries, and blueberries

For this take on an American classic, a refreshingly dry Collalbrigo Prosecco di Conegliano NV makes a lovely choice. The dry and spicy sparkling wine is just the thing for an afternoon (or any other time) cocktail party and won't compete with the moist, fluffy cupcakes.

To Make the Lemon Cupcakes

Preheat the oven to 350°F. Line 18 standard muffin cups with paper liners.

Sift together the flour, baking powder, and salt. In the bowl of a mixer, cream the butter, sugar, vanilla and lemon zest on medium speed until light and fluffy. Add the eggs, one at a time, beating well after each addition. On low speed, add the dry ingredients alternately with the milk in three batches, ending with the liquid. Fill each muffin cup three-quarters full with the batter. Bake for 18 to 20 minutes until a toothpick inserted into the center comes out clean. Remove the cupcakes from the pan and let cool completely on a wire rack.

To Make the Mixed Berries and Ricotta Cream

Using a whisk or in the bowl of a mixer fitted with a whisk attachment, whip the heavy cream to stiff peaks. Add the ricotta cheese and confectioners' sugar and whisk until smooth. Spread a thin layer of the ricotta cream on top of each cupcake. Arrange the berries over one-half of each cupcake and dust with confectioners' sugar. Spoon the ricotta cream into a pastry bag fitted with a medium round tip and pipe the cream on the uncovered side of each cupcake.

For the Mixed-Nut Cupcakes with Grand Marnier Cream

(makes 24 cupcakes)

1½ cups cake flour
1 tsp baking powder
½ tsp salt
1¾ cups granulated sugar
¼ cup whole almonds, blanched
¼ cup hazelnuts, peeled
¼ cup pistachios, shelled
¼ cup macadamia nuts
1½ cups (3 sticks) unsalted butter,
    at room temperature, 2 sticks of the butter
    cut into small pieces
1½ tsp vanilla extract
3 large eggs, at room temperature
¾ cup milk
3 large egg whites
¼ cup Grand Marnier or other orange-flavored
    liqueur
Finely grated zest of ½ large orange

To Make the Mixed-Nut Cupcakes

Preheat the oven to 350°F. Line 24 standard muffin cups with paper liners.

Sift together the flour, baking powder, and salt. Put 1 cup of the sugar, the almonds, hazelnuts, pistachios, and macadamia nuts into a food processor and pulse until they are finely ground.

In the bowl of a mixer, cream 1 stick of the butter, the sugar-nut mixture, and vanilla on medium speed until light and fluffy. Add the eggs, one at a time, mixing well after each addition. On low speed, add the dry ingredients alternately with the milk in three batches, ending with the liquid. Fill each muffin cup three-quarters full with the batter. Bake for 18 to 20 minutes until a toothpick inserted into the center comes out clean. Remove the cupcakes from the pan and let cool completely on a wire rack.

To Make the Grand Marnier Cream

Put the egg whites into a clean mixer bowl. Whisking constantly, gradually add the remaining ¾ cup sugar. Place the bowl over a pot of barely simmering water, making certain that the bottom of the bowl does not touch the water. Stir until the mixture is hot. Fit the mixer with a whisk attachment and whip the meringue until it holds tall, stiff, glossy peaks. Switch to a paddle attachment. Gradually add the cut-up butter to the meringue and beat until light and fluffy. Add the liqueur and orange zest and beat to incorporate. Spoon the cream into a pastry bag fitted with a medium star tip and pipe the cream on top of each cupcake.

Menus for Entertaining

Sunday Brunch

BERRINI (PAGE 12)

POTATO LATKES WITH SMOKED SALMON,
QUAIL EGGS, AND WATERCRESS (PAGE 26)

ARTICHOKE AND RADICCHIO CLAFOUTIS
(PAGE 45)

WALDORF MODERNE (PAGE 48)

ROASTED CHICKEN WITH GRAPES,
ARTICHOKES AND A CHICORY SALAD
(PAGE 112)

CHOCOLATE-RUM POTS DE CRÈME
WITH CINNAMON SACRISTAINS (PAGE 130)

Dinner with Friends

FROZEN SEABREEZE OR DANIEL'S MOJITO
(PAGE 16)

CHICKEN SATAY WITH SPICY PEANUT SAUCE
(PAGE 37)

WALDORF MODERNE (PAGE 48)

VIETNAMESE CRAB SPRING ROLLS (PAGE 75)

LAMB STEW WITH ROSEMARY AND ORANGE
(PAGE 99)

CHOCOLATE MOUSSE (PAGE 151)

Cocktail Reception

BERRINI (PAGE 12)

FROZEN SEABREEZE (PAGE 16)

DANIEL'S MOJITO (PAGE 16)

PARMESAN BASKETS WITH HERBED
GOAT CHEESE (PAGE 18)

BAKED LITTLENECK CLAMS WITH PROSCIUTTO
(PAGE 21)

CURRIED TUNA-STUFFED RADISHES (PAGE 22)

BLINI WITH CAVIAR AND CRÈME FRAÎCHE
(PAGE 25)

POTATO LATKES WITH SMOKED SALMON,
QUAIL EGGS, AND WATERCRESS (PAGE 26)

CHICKEN SATAY WITH SPICY PEANUT SAUCE
(PAGE 37)

VIETNAMESE CRAB SPRING ROLLS (PAGE 75)

SHRIMP CAKES WITH GOAT-CHEESE SAUCE
(PAGE 83)

TRIO OF CHOCOLATE ICE CREAMS (PAGE 144)

KIWI PÂTES DE FRUITS (PAGE 155)

TRIO OF CUPCAKES (PAGE 164)

Special Occasion

BERRINI (PAGE 12)

BLINI WITH CAVIAR AND CRÈME FRAÎCHE
(PAGE 25)

SAFFRON-INFUSED MUSSEL VELOUTÉ WITH
MUSSELS GRATINS (PAGE 54)

ORANGE-GLAZED SEA BREAM WITH TOMATO,
PESTO, AND FENNEL (PAGE 88)

DUCK À L'ORANGE (PAGE 109)

PASSION-FRUIT SOUFFLÉS WITH CARAMELIZED
PEAR-PASSION SAUCE (PAGE 147)

Holiday Menu

BERRINI (PAGE 12)

PARMESAN BASKETS WITH HERBED
GOAT CHEESE (PAGE 18)

STUFFED ARTICHOKES WITH DUNGENESS CRAB
AND CHANTERELLES (PAGE 42)

CARAMELIZED BAY SCALLOPS WITH
CLEMENTINES AND CAULIFLOWER (PAGE 62)

ROASTED VENISON WITH DATE SAUCE AND
ROOT VEGETABLES (PAGE 114)

PHYLLO APPLE TART WITH CALVADOS CRÈME
ANGLAISE (PAGE 136)

CRÈME BOULUD (PAGE 15)

Picnic

LOBSTER ROLL SANDWICH (PAGE 80)

SANDWICH BUNS
*Fresh roasted red peppers with anchovy fillets,
sliced ricotta salata, arugula, and basil leaves,
all sprinkled with extra-virgin olive oil.*

*Thin-sliced prosciutto, oven-baked red onion
wheels, and chopped fresh sage.*

*Mashed avocado, tomato slices, poached
shrimp, coriander, grated lime zest, olive oil,
and a dash of Tabasco.*
(PAGE 127)

MEDITERRANEAN TOMATO-LEMON TART
(PAGE 30)

MELON SALAD WITH LEMONGRASS SHRIMP
(PAGE 41)

MARINATED LAMB CHOPS WITH TWO SAUCES
(served cold) (PAGE 110)

CHAMONIX À L'ORANGE (PAGE 133)

Seasonal Menus

Spring

ASPARAGUS FOUR WAYS: STEAMED,
PAN ROASTED, GRATINÉED, AND TEMPURA
(PAGE 46)

SOFT SHELL CRABS WITH SORREL CREAM
(PAGE 65)

GUINEA HEN CASSEROLE WITH MORELS, FAVA
BEANS, AND FIDDLEHEAD FERNS (PAGE 96)

CHOCOLATE AND PISTACHIO CRÊPES SUZETTE
(PAGE 152)

CARROT MIRROR TART
WITH CARROT-CORIANDER CREAM (PAGE 32)

CLAM, TUNA, AND POTATO MARINIÈRE
(PAGE 76)

PEANUT-CRUSTED PORK TENDERLOIN
WITH SOUTHERN-STYLE VEGETABLES
(PAGE 102)

CHAMONIX À L'ORANGE (PAGE 133)

Summer

SEAFOOD À L'ORIENTALE (PAGE 79)

ASPARAGUS AND SHRIMP RISOTTO (PAGE 58)

STEAMED RED SNAPPER IN BAMBOO LEAVES
(PAGE 84)

CHERRY CLAFOUTIS (PAGE 160)

MEDITERRANEAN TOMATO-LEMON TART
(PAGE 30)

GRILLED TUNA WITH ROSEMARY-FENNEL
COULIS (PAGE 87)

MARINATED LAMB CHOPS WITH TWO SAUCES
(PAGE 110)

FROZEN STRAWBERRY SOUFFLÉS (PAGE 148)

Fall

SPICED BEEF BORSCHT (PAGE 50)

STUFFED SKATE WITH MUSSELS, POTATOES
AND SAFFRON BUTTER (PAGE 66)

SEED-CRUSTED RACK OF PORK
WITH CABBAGE-CRANBERRY COMPOTE
(PAGE 100)

BUTTERNUT SQUASH GRATIN (PAGE 120)

CHOCOLATE BREAD PUDDING
WITH DRIED FRUIT (PAGE 134)

———

EGGPLANT-WRAPPED SWORDFISH
WITH TOMATO AND MEYER LEMON (PAGE 72)

ROASTED CHICKEN WITH GRAPES,
ARTICHOKES, AND A CHICORY SALAD
(PAGE 112)

SPAGHETTI SQUASH WITH SAGE (PAGE 118)

PHYLLO APPLE TART WITH
CALVADOS CRÈME ANGLAISE (PAGE 136)

Winter

SAFFRON-INFUSED MUSSEL VELOUTÉ
WITH MUSSELS GRATINS (PAGE 54)

DANIEL'S CASUAL CASSOULET (PAGE 95)

CHOCOLATE-GINGER POUND CAKE
(PAGE 139)

———

POTATO AND REBLOCHON TART (PAGE 28)

ROASTED VENISON WITH DATE SAUCE
AND ROOT VEGETABLES (PAGE 114)

CHOCOLATE CAKES WITH NUT CARAMEL
(PAGE 143)

Pantry Basics

All-purpose flour
Bacon
Baking powder
Baking soda
Balsamic vinegar
Basil
Beans (dried or canned)
Brown sugar
Butter, unsalted
Carrots
Chicken or vegetable stock or broth
Cilantro (coriander leaves)
Cocoa powder, unsweetened, preferably
   Dutch process
Confectioners' sugar
Cornstarch
Crème fraîche
Dijon mustard
Dried bay leaves
Eggs
Extra-virgin olive oil
Flat-leaf parsley
Garlic
Heavy cream
Honey
Lemons
Mayonnaise
Milk

Nuts (assorted)
Onions
Parmesan cheese, fresh
Pasta, dried or fresh
Peppercorns, black and white
Potatoes
Red wine vinegar
Rice
Salt (coarse and fine)
Sesame oil
Shallots
Soy sauce
Spices (assorted)
Sugar
Tabasco sauce or chili flakes
Thyme sprigs
Tomato paste
Tomatoes
Vegetable oil
White-wine vinegar
Worcestershire sauce

This is not an all-inclusive list, but only a general guide.

Basic Equipment for the Kitchen

Baking sheets
Basting brushes
Blender
Blender, immersion
Cake and loaf pans
Cheesecloth
Chinois
Colander
Custard cups, soufflé cups or ramekins
Cutting boards
Dry measuring cups
Dutch oven or large casserole
Electric knife
Food processor
Fork, long-tined
Ice cream scoops
Kitchen string
Kitchen timer
Knives
    8-inch knife
    10-inch knife
    12 inch knife
    4-inch paring knife
    6-inch paring knife
    a long thin-bladed slicing knife
    a serrated slicing knife
Liquid measuring cups
Mandoline
Measuring spoons
Mixer, stand
Mixing bowls
Parchment paper
Pastry bag and tip
Pastry or dough scraper
Pepper mill
Ring molds or round cutters
Roasting pan

Rolling pin
Sauce ladles
Saucepans
Scale
Scissors or kitchen shears
Sharpening steel and electric knife sharpener
Skillets or sauté pans including a non-stick skillet
Spatulas, Metal
    Spatulas of the pancake-turner variety with a
        long handle and a flipper that's offset
    Peltex, a slotted flexible spatula with a shorter
        handle and somewhat angled flipper
    Thin offset Spatulas, 10 inches long
        (icing spatulas)
Spatulas, rubber
Spatulas, wooden
Spoons, metal
    Large with long handles
    Slotted with long handles
Spoons, wooden
Stainless-steel double-mesh strainers
Stockpots
Tart pans and tart rings
Thermometers
    a deep-fat frying thermometer
    an instant-read thermometer
    an oven thermometer
Tongs with scalloped or rounded pincers
Vegetable peelers
    Swivel-blade vegetable peeler
    Stationary-blade vegetable peeler
Whisks
    Sauce whisk
    Balloon whisk
Zester/Grater

This is not an all-inclusive list, but only a general guide.

Kitchen Source Guide

EQUIPMENT

DANIEL BOULUD KITCHEN (DBK)
www.bloomingdales.com
www.chefscatalog.com
www.amazon.com
For more information, visit www.danielnyc.com
*Professional quality knives, enameled cast Iron
cookware, stainless steel cookware, kitchen tools*

ALL-CLAD METALCRAFTERS
Ph: 800-ALL-CLAD
www.allclad.com
Top-quality cookware

J.B. PRINCE
36 East 31st Street, 11th Floor
New York, NY 10016
Ph: 212-683-3553 | Fax: 212-683-4488
www.jbprince.com
*Knives, mixers, blenders, small electrical tools,
baking pans, and assorted cookware*

SABATIER
Ph: 516-794-3355
Fine-quality knives

KITCHEN AID
www.kitchenaid.com
Fine-quality stand mixers

NEW YORK CAKE AND BAKING DISTRIBUTORS, INC.
56 West 22nd Street
New York, NY 10010
www.nycake.com
*Cake-decorating and baking equipment and supplies,
including chocolate, sheet gelatin, and marzipan*

WILLIAMS-SONOMA
To locate a store, please call 877 812 6235
  or visit www.williams-sonoma.com
*Assorted cookware, small electrical equipment and
tools, bakeware, dinnerware, glassware*

INGREDIENTS

BROWNE TRADING CO.
260 Commercial Street
Portland, ME 04101
Ph: 800-944-7848 | Fax: 207-766-2404
www.browne-trading.com
*Daniel Boulud's Private Stock Caviar and
Smoked Salmon, lobsters, Peekytoe crabmeat,
crayfish, oysters, salt cod, smoked beluga
sturgeon, diver and other sea scallops,
and other pristine fish and seafood*

D'ARTAGNAN, INC.
Ph: 800-DARTAGN or 973-344-0565
www.dartagnan.com
*Duck-breast prosciutto, duck confit, foie gras,
partridge, guinea hen, pheasant, squab, venison, and
other game, demi-glace, and wild mushrooms*

KALUSTYAN'S
123 Lexington Avenue
New York, NY 10016
Ph: 212-685-3451 | Fax: 212-683-8458
www.kalustyans.com
*Specializing in Middle Eastern spices and foods as
well as ingredients from Bangladesh, Belgium, China,
Egypt, England, France, Germany, Greece, Guatemala,
Indonesia, Israel, Italy, Japan, Jordan, Lebanon,
Morocco, the Philippines, Syria, Thailand, Turkey, and
the West Indies, among other countries.*

King Arthur Flour
Norwich, Vermont
Ph: 800-827-6839 | www.kingarthurflour.com
Premium flours: all-purpose, bread, whole wheat, yeast, and other baking ingredients and supplies

Murray's Cheese Shop
257 Bleecker Street
New York, NY 10014
Ph: 888-692-4339 | www.murrayscheese.com
Fine domestic and imported cheeses

Valronha Inc.
1801 Avenue of the Stars, Suite 829
Los Angeles, CA 90067
Ph: 310-277-0401 | www.valrhona.com
Manufacturer of professional-quality French chocolate

Buon Italia
75 Ninth Avenue
New York, NY 10011
Ph: 212-633-9090 | Fax: 212-633-9717
www.buonitalia.com
Specializing in Italian food products such as pasta flour, olive oil, cheese, and meats

Hudson Valley Foie Gras
80 Brooks Road
Ferndale, NY 12734
Ph: 845-292-2500 | Fax: 845-292-3009
www.hudsonvalleyfoiegras.com
Specializing in duck products, including foie gras

Jamison Farm
171 Jamison Lane
Latrobe, PA 15650
Ph: 800-237-5262 | Fax: 724-837-2287
www.jamisonfarm.com
Farm-raised Pennsylvania lamb and prepared foods

Salumeria Biellese
378 Eighth Avenue
New York, NY 10001
Ph: 212-736-7376 | Fax: 212-736-1093
Speck ham, sausages, chorizo and charcuterie

Da Rosario
Ph: 800-281-2330 | www.shopdarosario.com
Truffles and caviar

International Spice House
315 West John Street
Hicksville, NY 11802
Ph: 516-942-7248 | Fax: 516-942-7249
www.spicehouseint.com
Chili peppers and Mexican spices

Schaller & Weber
22-35 46th Street
Astoria, NY 11105
Ph: 800-847-4115 | Fax: 718-956-9157
www.schallerweber.com
Pork belly, smoked German-style charcuterie, and sausage

Dean & Deluca
575 Broadway
New York, NY 10012
www.deandeluca.com
Cookware and fine foods including caviar, quail eggs, charcuterie, fresh meats, fresh seafoods, smoked and cured fish, cheeses, oils, coffee, chocolate, herbs, and spices

Katagiri & Co., Inc.
224 East 59th Street
New York, NY 10022
Ph: 212-755-3566 | Fax: 212-752-4197
www.katagiri.com
Matcha (powdered Japanese green tea)

Credits

COVER: Plate: Simon Pearce; glass: Hable Construction; placemat: Simon Pearce.

pp. 2–3. Orange, clear and pink glass: Hable Construction.

p. 10. Glasses: ABC Carpet & Home; vase: Hable Construction; plate and bowls: Armani Casa; placemat: Nancy Koltes; tablecloth: The Silk Trading Co.

p. 13. Flute: Movado; cruet: MoMA Design Store; napkin: Crate & Barrel.

p. 14. Glasses: MoMA NY Design Store; placemat: Crate & Barrel.

p. 17 (right). Flute: Calvin Klein Home Collection.

p. 19. Plate: Takashimaya New York; placemat: Broadway Panhandler.

p. 23. Placemat: Broadway Panhandler.

p. 24. Shells, spoon, glasses, tray: Takashimaya New York.

p. 27. Plates and napkin: Crate & Barrel.

p. 29. Plate: Crate & Barrel; glass: Nancy Koltes.

p. 31. Bowl and cloth: Crate & Barrel.

p. 32. Plate: Takashimaya New York; placemat: Nancy Koltes.

p. 35. Placemat: Simon Pearce.

p. 36. Basket and tray: Simon Pearce.

p. 39. Plate: Bernardaud New York; fork: Kar'ikter; placemat: Global Table.

p. 40. Bowls: Nancy Koltes; placemat: Crate & Barrel.

p. 43. Plates: Bernardaud New York; glass: ABC Carpet & Home; oil cruet: MoMA Design Store; placemat and napkin: Broadway Panhandler.

p. 44. Plate and placemat: Simon Pearce; glass: Nancy Koltes; vases: ABC Carpet & Home.

p. 47. Plate: Aero.

p. 48. Bowl: Simon Pearce; dip bowls: MoMA Design Store; glass: Armani Casa; placemat and napkin: Broadway Panhandler.

p. 50. Bowl: Crate & Barrel; spoon, placemat, and napkin: Nancy Koltes.

p. 52. Plate: Crate & Barrel; bowl: MoMA Design Store; glass, pitcher, and placemat: Nancy Koltes.

p. 55. Bowl, placemat, and napkin: Simon Pearce; spoon: MoMA Design Store.

p. 56. Bowl and vase: Hable Construction; tray and napkin: Crate & Barrel.

p. 59. Plates: Takashimaya New York; cloth: Nancy Koltes.

p. 60. Bowls: Aero; tablecloth: The Silk Trading Co.

p. 63. Plates and bowl: Broadway Panhandler; placemat: Nancy Koltes.

p. 64. Glass tray and dip bowl: Crate & Barrel.

p. 67. Round baking pans: Broadway Panhandler; placemat: Crate & Barrel.

p. 69. Plate: Global Table; placemat: ABC Carpet & Home.

p. 70. Plate: Global Table; fork: Pavillon Christofle; vase and tablecloth: ABC Carpet & Home; glass: Nancy Koltes.

p. 73. Plates and glass: Aero; napkin: Broadway Panhandler.

p. 74. Plate: Broadway Panhandler; bowl and placemat: : Crate & Barrel.

p. 77. Plate and bowl: Room One; spoon: Pavillon Christofle; glass: ABC Carpet & Home; tablecloth: ABC Carpet & Home.

p. 78. Plates: Global Table; glass: Pavillon Christofle; placemat: Crate & Barrel; napkin: Nancy Koltes.

p. 81. Placemat: Crate & Barrel; cloth: Broadway Panhandler.

p. 82. Slate: Crate & Barrel; bowls: ABC Carpet & Home.

p. 86. Plate, glass, and placemat: Aero; bowl: ABC Carpet & Home; napkin: Broadway Panhandler.

p. 89. Plates and placemats: Crate & Barrel; glasses: Simon Pearce.

p. 90. Pitcher, plates and wine glasses: Nancy Koltes; striped water glass and tablecloth: ABC Carpet & Home.

p. 93. Antique Indian Silver Pooja Ceremonial Plate: Jacques Carcanagues Gallery.

p. 94. Bowl: Crate & Barrel; cloth: Broadway Panhandler.

p. 97. Plate: Simon Pearce; fork: Pavillon Christofle; glass: Hable Construction; placemat: Simon Pearce.

p. 98. Bowl: Global Table; fork and spoon: Takashimaya New York; Glass: ABC Carpet & Home; placemat: Crate & Barrel.

p. 101. Plate: Sara; glass and napkin: ABC Carpet & Home; placemat: Lâle.

p. 102. Plates: Bernardaud New York; glass: ABC Carpet & Home; tablecloth: Crate & Barrel.

p. 104. Plate: ABC Carpet & Home; baking pan: Crate & Barrel; napkin: Nancy Koltes.

p. 107. Plate: Aero.

p. 108. Serving fork and knife: Daniel Boulud Knife Collection; cloth: Crate & Barrel.

p. 111. Plate and bowl: Armani Casa; fork and knife: Takashimaya New York; placemat and napkin: Simon Pearce.

p. 113. Plates: Broadway Panhandler; silverware: Takashimaya New York; glass: Armani Casa; placemat: Simon Pearce.

p. 115. Plate and glass: Sara; fork and knife: Takashimaya New York; placemat: Global Table.

p. 116. Placemat: Jamson's; cloth: Crate & Barrel.

p. 119. Plates and placemat: Simon Pearce.

p. 122. Glasses: Simon Pearce; placemat: MoMA Design Store.

p. 126. Board and placemat: Simon Pearce; glass: ABC Carpet & Home.

p. 131. Bowls: Broadway Panhandler; table runner: Simon Pearce; napkin ring: Nancy Koltes.

p. 132. Plate: Global Table; bowl: Global Table; glass bowl: Lâle; placemat: Broadway Panhandler.

p. 135. Plate and bowl: Global Table.

p. 137. Plate: Takashimaya New York; napkin: Crate & Barrel.

p. 138. Plate and coffee set: Bernardaud New York; placemat: MoMA Design Store.

p. 142. Plates and placemats: Crate & Barrel; glasses: Simon Pearce.

p. 145. Pillow: ABC Carpet & Home.

p. 146. Ramekin: Broadway Panhandler; placemat: Sara; napkin: Crate & Barrel.

p. 149. Napkin: Crate & Barrel.

p. 150. Plate and bowl: Nancy Koltes; spoon: Pavillon Christofle; bowl (background): Lâle.

p. 153. Plate: Bernardaud New York; placemat: Global Table.

p. 154. Plate: Armani Casa.

p. 157. Glass: Bernardaud New York; tray: Takashimaya New York; placemat: Simon Pearce.

p. 158. Bowl, plate, and mug: ABC Carpet & Home; spoon: Kar'ikter; tray: Aero.

p. 161. Baking pan: Crate & Barrel; spoon: Nancy Koltes; placemat and napkin: Nancy Koltes.

p. 162. Plate: Pearl River; glass: Nancy Koltes; placemat: Takashimaya New York.

p. 165. Plate: Armani Casa; placemat: Global Table.

Objects not credited belong to Daniel Boulud.

Thank you to all the New York stores that provided us with the above objects.

Tableware Source Guide

ABC CARPET & HOME
888 Broadway, New York, NY 10003
Ph: 212-473-3000 | www.abchome.com

AERO STUDIOS
132 Spring Street, New York, NY 10012
Ph: 212-966-1500 | www.aerostudios.com

ARMANI CASA
97 Greene Street, New York, NY 10012
Ph: 212-334-1271 | www.armanicasa.com

BERNARDAUD NEW YORK
499 Park Avenue, New York, NY 10022
Ph: 212-371-4300 | www.bernardaud.net

BROADWAY PANHANDLER
477 Broome Street, New York, NY 10013
Ph: 212-966-3434 | www.broadwaypanhandler.com

CRATE & BARREL
Locations nationwide
www.crateandbarrel.com

GLOBAL TABLE
107-109 Sullivan Street, New York, NY 10012
Ph: 212-431-5839 | www.globaltable.com

HABLE CONSTRUCTION
230 Elizabeth Street, New York, NY 10012
Ph: 212-343-8555 | www.hableconstruction.com

JACQUES CARCANAGUES GALLERY
21 Greene Street, New York, NY 10013
Ph: 212-925-8110 | e-mail: carcan@rcn.com

JAMSON'S
316 Bleecker Street, New York, NY 10014
Ph: 212-255-6420

KAR'IKTER
19 Prince Street, New York, NY 10012
Ph: 212-274-1966 | www.karikter.com

LÂLE FOR HOME
200 Mott Street, New York, NY 10012
Ph: 212-941-7641 | www.lalenyc.com

MoMA DESIGN STORE (SOHO)
81 Spring Street, New York, NY 10012
Ph: 646-613-1367 | www.momastore.org

MOVADO
138 Spring Street, New York, NY 10012
Ph: 212-431-0249 | www.movado.com

NANCY KOLTES
31 Spring Street, New York, NY 10021
Ph: 212-219-2271 | www.nancykoltes.com

PAVILLON CHRISTOFLE
680 Madison Avenue, New York, NY 10021
Ph: 212-308-9390 | www.christofle.com

ROOM ONE
229 Mott Street, New York, NY 10012
Ph: 212-625-9444 | www.room001.com

SARA
952 Lexington Avenue, New York, NY 10021
Ph: 212-772-3243 | www.saranyc.com

SIMON PEARCE
120 Wooster Street, New York, NY 10012
Ph: 212-334-2393 | www.simonpearce.com

TAKASHIMAYA NEW YORK
693 Fifth Avenue, New York, NY 10022
Ph: 212-350-0100 | www.ginza-west.co.jp/ny.htm

THE SILK TRADING CO.
888 Broadway, Lower Level, New York, NY 10003
Ph: 212-966-5464 | www.silktrading.com

Behind the Scenes

Acknowledgments

My most sincere thanks to the people who made this book possible

Dorothée Walliser, my publisher, and Jessica Dheere, my editor at Filipacchi Publishing, for adding so much to the text and design of this project—your expertise is greatly admired and appreciated.

Photographer Peter Medilek and his assistant, Kiyoharu Goto, for capturing the exact mood and style of my food.

Patricia Fabricant for her sophisticated layouts and for the insight she brought to all our shoots.

Stylist Sonja Jurgens, for seeking and finding such perfect, interesting tableware and accessories for each and every dish.

Talented chefs Cyrille Allannic, Rémy Fünfrock, and Lior Lev Sercarz, for testing and styling every recipe.

Mark Fiorentino for his beautiful breads.

Deborah Mintcheff for her exhaustive recipe editing.

Katherine Yang, my Jill-of-all-Trades, for pouring her heart and soul into every aspect of this project, from start to finish.

Jean Luc Le Dû, my gifted sommelier at DANIEL, for the wonderful wine pairings and descriptions to match my food.

Margaret Russell, Miranda Crowell, and the staff at ELLE DECOR for years of support and creative input into my recipe column for the magazine. I am grateful to them for making this book a reality.

Alex Lee, Andrew Carmellini, Jean François Bruel, Fabrizio Salerni, Patrice Martineau, Eddy Leroux, Eric Bertoïa, Sandro Micheli, Anthony Francis, Celia Laurent, Ginette Vrod, Arezki "Toto" Ourzdine, Michael Lawrence, Jed Davis, Jean-Pierre François, Georgette Farkas, Hilary Tolman, Gail Simmons, and Elizabeth Grey Keenan; and the rest of my staff at DANIEL, Café Boulud, and DB Bistro Moderne in New York for their hard work and patience.

Index by Season

FALL
Artichoke and Radicchio Clafoutis, 45
Butternut Squash Gratin, 120
Chocolate Bread Pudding with Dried Fruit, 134
Creamy Polenta with Porcini, Parmesan
    and Oregano, 121
Orange-Glazed Sea Bream with Tomato,
    Pesto and Fennel, 88
Passion-Fruit Soufflés with Caramelized
    Pear-Passion Sauce, 147
Roasted Chicken with Grapes, Artichokes
    and a Chicory Salad, 112
Roasted Turkey Breast with Endive,
    Apple, and Walnuts, 104
Seed-Crusted Rack of Pork with
    Cabbage-Cranberry Compote, 100
Spaghetti Squash with Sage, 118
Spiced Beef Borscht, 50
Squash Panna Cotta with Cranberry
    Compote and Walnut Tuiles, 162
Stuffed Skate with Mussels, Potatoes,
    and Saffron Butter, 66
Waldorf Moderne, 48

FALL/WINTER
Caramelized Bay Scallops with
    Clementines and Cauliflower, 62
Curried Tuna–Stuffed Radishes, 22
Roasted Venison with Date Sauce
    and Root Vegetables, 114
Phyllo Apple Tart with Calvados
    Crème Anglaise, 136

WINTER
Alsatian Potato Gratin, 117
Daniel's Casual Cassoulet, 95
Duck à l'Orange, 109
Lamb Stew with Rosemary and Orange, 99
Pineapple and Coconut Givré, 140
Potato and Reblochon Tart, 28

Spiced Chocolate Soup with
    Caramel Whipped Cream, 159

SPRING
Asparagus and Shrimp Risotto, 58
Asparagus Four Ways: Steamed, Pan
    Roasted, Gratinéed, and Tempura , 46
Carrot Mirror Tart with Carrot-
    Coriander Cream, 32
Clam, Tuna, and Potato Marinière, 76
Four-Greens Tart, 34
Penne with Morels, and Spring Peas,
    Bacon, and Eggs, 57
Soft-Shell Crabs with Sorrel Cream, 65
Spring Root-Vegetable Potage with Sorrel, 53

SPRING/SUMMER
Grilled Tuna with Rosemary-
    Fennel Coulis, 87
Guinea Hen Casserole with Morels,
    Fava Beans, and Fiddlehead Ferns, 96
Peanut-Crusted Pork Tenderloin with
    Southern-Style Vegetables, 102
Spicy Sea Bass with Olive-Crushed
    Potatoes, 71
Stuffed Artichokes with Dungeness
    Crab and Chanterelles, 42
Yogurt, Rhubarb and Lime Dressing, 120

SUMMER
Berrini, 12
Catalan Stuffed Tomatoes, 38
Cherry Clafoutis, 160
Eggplant-Wrapped Swordfish with
    Tomato and Meyer Lemon, 72
Frozen Strawberry Soufflés, 148
Lobster Roll Sandwich, 80
Marinated Lamb Chops with Two Sauces, 110
Mediterranean Tomato-Lemon Tart, 30
Melon Salad with Lemongrass Shrimp, 41

Rice Pudding Parfaits with Raspberries
and Green-Tea Cream, 156
Saffron-Infused Mussel Velouté with
Mussels Gratins, 54
Seafood à l'Orientale, 79
Steamed Red Snapper in Bamboo Leaves, 84
Vietnamese Crab Spring Rolls, 75

YEAR-ROUND

Baked Littleneck Clams with Prosciutto, 21
Blini with Caviar and Crème Fraîche, 25
Chamonix à l'Orange, 133
Chicken Satay with Spicy Peanut Sauce, 37
Chocolate and Pistachio Crêpes Suzette, 152
Chocolate Cakes with Nut Caramel, 143
Chocolate Mousse, 151
Chocolate-Ginger Pound Cake, 139
Chocolate-Rum Pots de Crème with
Cinnamon Sacristains, 130
Classic Hamburger and Three Variations, 92
Cod Lyonnaise, Dijonnaise, and Bordelaise, 68
Crème Boulud, 15
Daniel's Mojito, 16
Frozen Seabreeze, 16
Kiwi Pâtes de Fruits, 155
Mini Baguettes & Butter Balls, 128
Parmesan Baskets with Herbed
Goat Cheese, 18
Peppered Côte de Boeuf with Pommes
Pont Neuf and Watercress Salad, 106
Potato Latkes with Smoked Salmon,
Quail Eggs, and Watercress, 26
Sandwich Buns, 127
Shrimp Cakes with Goat-Cheese Sauce, 83
Speck Ham and Sage Boules, 124
Trio of Chocolate Ice Creams, 144
Trio of Cupcakes, 164

Index of Wines and Spirits

Aiguilhe, Château d', 109
Albarino, 21
Alsatian wines, 22, 25, 28, 47, 75, 80
Argentine wines, 96
Au Bon Climat, 87, 112
Aubuisières, Domaine des, 45
Australian wines, 96, 134

Bandol, 80
Banyuls, 143
Barossa, 134
Basa, 18
beer and ale, 79, 80, 93
Blanck, Paul, Domaine, 28, 75
Bongran, Domaine la, 72
Bordeaux, 66, 68, 109, 147
Burgundy, 26, 57, 68, 72, 76

Cabernet Sauvignon, 107
Cadallora, La, 22
Caillebourdin, Domaine, 65
Caillot, Domaine, 57, 76
California wines, 41, 47, 50, 62, 71, 85, 87, 95, 99,
    100, 103, 107, 109, 112, 115, 130, 151
Calvados, 159
Camut, 159
Canadian wines, 160
Carbonnieux, Château, 66
Carneros, Domaine, 151
Cave Spring, 160
Cerdon du Bugey, 157
Chablis, 26
Champagne, 145
Chardonnay, 26, 41, 62, 72, 76
Chenin Blanc, 45, 58, 137
Chilean wines, 41
Chimay, 93
cider, 49, 104
Clos Naudin, Domaine du, 37
Clos de la Coulée de Serrant, Domaine du, 58
Clos Roche Blanche Touraine, 33
Códax, Martín, 21
Cognac, 155
Cold Heaven Winery, 85
Collalbrigo, 166

Condrieu, 30
Corona, 93
Coteaux du Languedoc, 115
Coteaux du Layon, 137
Côte Rôtie, 107
Cristom, 117

Disznoko, 133
Dominio de Atauta, 38
Donnhoff, Weingut, 79
Duché de Longueville, 49

Eau de Vie, 25

Felline, 110
Fonseca, 152
Foreau, Domaine, 53

Gavoty, Domaine, 43
German wines, 33, 37
Gewurztraminer, 22, 28
Gini, 49
Goisot, 68
Graves, 66
Guigal, Etienne, 107

Hanzell, 62
Haut-Médoc, 68
Hermitage, 88
Hine, 155
Hornsby, George, 104
Hungarian wines, 133

Italian wines, 22, 35, 49, 99, 110, 140, 160, 163, 166

Jones, Trevor, 134

Kendall-Jackson, 41

Languedoc wines, 55, 115
late-harvest wines, 130, 140, 147, 160
Linne Colado, 130
Lis Neris, 35
Loire Valley wines, 37, 45, 53, 58, 65, 137

Mâcon, 68
Mâcon-Villages, 72
Manoir de Kinkiz, 104
Manzano, Fattoria di, 110
Maremma, 140
Mas Daumas-Gassac, 55
Merlot, 96, 109
Mersault, 57
Mette, 25
Michel, Louis, 26
Monbazillac, 147
Montus, Château, 95
Müller-Catoir, 33
Muscat, 47

Napa Valley wines, 50, 107, 115
New York wines, 49, 83

OB, 93
OP Vodka, 25
Oregon wines, 117

Parcé, Dr., 143
Paso Robles, 47
Phelps, Joseph, 107
Pibarnon, Château de, 80
Pierre-Bise, Château, 137
Pinot Blanc, 80, 87
Pinot Gris, 75, 87
Pinot Noir, 112, 117
port, tawny, 134, 152
Pouilly-Fumé, 65
Prieuré Saint-Jean de Bébian, 115
Primitivo di Manduria, 110
Prosecco, 160, 166
Provençal wines, 43, 55, 80, 115

Qupé, 103

Ravenswood, 99
Renardat-Fache, 139
Rhône Valley wines, 30, 88, 107, 157
Ridge, 95
Riesling, 33, 37, 49, 79, 83, 160

Rosemount Estate, 96
rosé wines, 43, 145

Sangiovese, 115
Santa Rita, 41
Sauvignon Blanc, 33, 35, 41, 68, 71, 140, 147
Seghesio, 100
Selbach-Oster, 37
Semillon, 140, 147
Shiraz, 96
Sierra Nevada Pale Ale, 80
Soave, 49
Sociando-Mallet, Château, 68
Spanish wines, 18, 21, 38
sparkling wines, 139, 145, 151, 157, 160, 166
Storybook Mountain Vineyards, 50
Swanson, 115
Syrah, 103, 110

Tablas Creek, 47
Taittinger, 145
Tannat, 95
Tardieu-Laurent, 30
Taurino, Dr. Cosimo, 99
tawny port, 134, 152
Taylor, 152
Thevenet, Jean, 68
Tirecul, Château, 147
Tokaji, 133
Trimbach, Domaine, 80
Tsing Tao, 79

Vin Santo, 163
Viognier, 30, 85
Vouvray, 37, 45, 53

Weinert, Bodega, 96
Westerly Vineyards, 71
Wiemer, Hermann J., 49, 83

Zind-Humbrecht, Domaine, 47
Zinfandel, 50, 99, 100, 104, 130

Index of Recipes and Ingredients

A

Alsatian potato gratin, *116*, 117

appetizers. *See* starters and small bites

apple:
    gelée, in Waldorf moderne, *48*, 48–49
    roasted turkey breast with endive, walnuts and,
        104, *105*
    tart, phyllo, with Calvados crème anglaise,
        136–37, *137*

artichoke(s):
    and radicchio clafoutis, *44*, 45
    roasted chicken with grapes and, 112–13, *113*
    stuffed, with Dungeness crab and chanterelles,
        42–43, *43*

arugula, in four-greens tart, 34–35, *35*

Asian:
    burger, 92
    lobster sandwich, 80

asparagus:
    four ways (steamed, pan roasted, gratinéed,
        and tempura), 46–47, *47*
    and shrimp risotto, 58, *59*

B

bacon:
    Alsatian potato gratin, *116*, 117
    penne with morels, spring peas, eggs and, 56, *57*

bamboo leaves, steamed red snapper in, 84–85, *85*

beans:
    cannellini, in Daniel's casual cassoulet, *94*, 95
    cranberry, in seafood à l'Orientale, *78*, 79
    fava, guinea hen casserole with morels, fiddlehead
        ferns and, *96*, 97

beef:
    borscht, spiced, 50, *51*
    hamburger, classic, and three variations, 92–93, *93*
    peppered côte de boeuf with pommes Pont Neuf
        and watercress salad, 106–7, *107*

beets, in spiced beef borscht, 50, *51*

berries. *See also specific berries*
    mixed, lemon cupcakes with ricotta cream and,
        165, 166

berrini, 12, *13*

blini with caviar and crème fraîche, *24*, 25

borscht, spiced beef, 50, *51*

boules, speck ham and sage, 124–25, *125*

bread(s), 123–29
    mini-baguettes and butter balls, 128–29, *129*
    pudding, chocolate, with dried fruit, 134, *135*
    sandwich buns, 126, 127
    speck ham and sage boules, 124–25, *125*

broccoli rabe, in Southern-style vegetables, *102*,
    102–3

buns, sandwich, 126, 127

butter balls (breads), 128–29, *129*

butternut squash:
    gratin, 120
    panna cotta with cranberry compote and walnut
        tuiles, *162*, 162–63

C

cabbage-cranberry compote, 100, *101*

cakes:
    chamonix à l'orange, *132*, 133
    chocolate, with nut caramel, *142*, 143
    chocolate-ginger pound, *138*, 139
    trio of cupcakes, 164–67, *165*

Calvados crème anglaise, 136, *137*

cannellini beans, in Daniel's casual cassoulet, *94*, 95

caramel:
    nut, chocolate cakes with, *142*, 143
    whipped cream, *158*, 159

carrot mirror tart with carrot-coriander cream,
    32, 32–33

cassoulet, Daniel's casual, *94*, 95

Catalan stuffed tomatoes, 38, *39*

cauliflower, caramelized bay scallops with
    clementines and, 62, *63*

caviar, blini with crème fraîche and, *24*, 25

chamonix à l'orange, *132*, 133

champagne, in berrini, 12, *13*

chanterelles, stuffed artichokes with Dungeness
    crab and, 42–43, *43*

cherry clafoutis, 160, *161*

chicken:
    roasted, with grapes, artichokes, and a chicory

salad, 112–13, *113*
satay with spicy peanut sauce, *36, 37*
chicory salad, 112–13, *113*
chocolate:
　bread pudding with dried fruit, 134, *135*
　cakes with nut caramel, *142, 143*
　coffee cupcakes with mocha ganache and
　　mascarpone cream, 164, *165*
　ginger pound cake, *138, 139*
　ice creams, trio of, 144–45, *145*
　mousse, *150,* 151
　and pistachio crêpes suzette, 152–53, *153*
　rum pots de crème with cinnamon sacristains,
　　130, *131*
　soup, spiced, with caramel whipped cream, *158,* 159
cinnamon sacristains, 130, *131*
clafoutis:
　artichoke and radicchio, *44, 45*
　cherry, 160, *161*
clam(s):
　baked littleneck, with prosciutto, *20,* 21
　littleneck, in seafood à l'Orientale, *78, 79*
tuna, and potato marinière, 76, *77*
clementines, caramelized bay scallops with
　cauliflower and, *62, 63*
cocktails, 12–17
　berrini, *12, 13*
　crème Boulud, *14,* 15
　mojito, Daniel's, *16, 17*
　seabreeze, frozen, *16, 17*
coconut and pineapple givré, 140–41, *141*
cod Lyonnaise, Dijonnaise, and Bordelaise, 68–69, *69*
coffee-chocolate cupcakes with mocha ganache and
　mascarpone cream, 164, *165*
compotes:
　cranberry, *162,* 162–63
　cabbage-cranberry, 100, *101*
　orange, *132, 133*
côte de boeuf, peppered, with pommes Pont Neuf
　and watercress salad, 106–7, *107*
crab(s):
　Dungeness, stuffed artichokes with chanterelles
　　and, 42–43, *43*

soft shell, with sorrel cream, *64, 65*
spring rolls, Vietnamese, *74, 75*
cranberry(ies):
　cabbage compote, 100, *101*
　compote, *162,* 162–63
　frozen seabreeze, *16, 17*
cranberry beans, in seafood à l'Orientale, *78, 79*
cream:
　caramel, whipped, *158,* 159
　carrot-coriander, *32, 33*
　Grand Marnier, *165, 167*
　mascarpone, 164, *165*
　ricotta, *165,* 166
　sorrel, *64, 65*
crème anglaise, Calvados, 136, *137*
crème Boulud, *14,* 15
crêpes suzette, chocolate and pistachio, 152–53, *153*
cupcakes, 164–67
　chocolate-coffee, with mocha ganache and
　　mascarpone cream, 164, *165*
　lemon, with mixed berries and ricotta cream,
　　165, 166
　mixed-nut, with Grand Marnier cream, *165, 167*
curried tuna–stuffed radishes, *22, 23*

D
dandelion, in four-greens tart, 34–35, *35*
date sauce, roasted venison with root vegetables
　and, 114–15, *115*
desserts, 130–67
　chamonix à l'orange, *132,* 133
　cherry clafoutis, 160, *161*
　chocolate and pistachio crêpes suzette, 152–53,
　　153
　chocolate bread pudding with dried fruit, 134, *135*
　chocolate cakes with nut caramel, *142,* 143
　chocolate-ginger pound cake, *138, 139*
　chocolate ice creams, trio of, 144–45, *145*
　chocolate mousse, *150,* 151
　chocolate-rum pots de crème with cinnamon
　　sacristains, 130, *131*
　chocolate soup, spiced, with caramel whipped
　　cream, *158,* 159

cupcakes, trio of, 164–67, *165*
kiwi pâtes de fruits, *154, 155*
passion-fruit soufflés with caramelized pear-
    passion sauce, *146,* 147
phyllo apple tart with Calvados crème anglaise,
    136–37, *137*
pineapple and coconut givré, 140–41, *141*
rice pudding parfaits with raspberries and green-
    tea cream, 156–57, *157*
squash panna cotta with cranberry compote and
    walnut tuiles, *162,* 162–63
strawberry soufflés, frozen, 148, *149*
dressing, yogurt, rhubarb, and lime, 120
dried fruit, chocolate bread pudding with, 134, *135*
duck:
    cassoulet, Daniel's casual, *94,* 95
    à l'orange, *108,* 109

E

eggplant-wrapped swordfish with tomato and
    Meyer lemon, 72, *73*
eggs:
    penne with morels, spring peas, bacon and, *56, 57*
    quail, potato latkes with smoked salmon,
        watercress and, *26, 27*
endive, roasted turkey breast with apple, walnuts
    and, 104, *105*

F

fava beans, guinea hen casserole with morels,
    fiddlehead ferns and, 96, *97*
fennel:
    orange-glazed sea bream with tomato,
        pesto and, 88, *89*
rosemary coulis, grilled tuna with, 86, *87*
fiddlehead ferns, guinea hen casserole with morels,
    fava beans and, 96, *97*
fish and shellfish entrées, 61–89
    clam, tuna, and potato marinière, 76, *77*
    cod Lyonnaise, Dijonnaise, and Bordelaise, 68–69,
        69
    crabs, soft shell with sorrel cream, *64, 65*
    crab spring rolls, Vietnamese, *74, 75*

lobster roll sandwich, 80–81, *81*
red snapper, steamed, in bamboo leaves, 84–85,
    85
scallops, caramelized bay, with clementines and
    cauliflower, 62, *63*
sea bass with olive-crushed potatoes, spicy, 70, *71*
sea bream, orange-glazed, with tomato, pesto and
    fennel, 88, *89*
seafood à l'Orientale, 78, *79*
shrimp cakes with goat-cheese sauce, 82, *83*
skate, stuffed, with mussels, potatoes, and saffron
    butter, 66, *67*
swordfish, eggplant-wrapped, with tomato and
    Meyer lemon, 72, *73*
tuna, grilled, with rosemary-fennel coulis, 86, *87*
four-greens tart, 34–35, *35*
Frangelico, in crème Boulud, *14, 15*
frisée (chicory) salad, 112–13, *113*

G

ganache, mocha, 164, *165*
ginger(ed):
    chocolate pound cake, *138, 139*
    tomato sauce, 110, *111*
givré, pineapple and coconut, 140–41, *141*
goat cheese:
    herbed, Parmesan baskets with, 18, *19*
    sauce, shrimp cakes with, 82, *83*
Grand Marnier cream, *165,* 167
grapefruit, in frozen seabreeze, 16, *17*
grapes, roasted chicken with artichokes and,
    112–13, *113*
gratins:
    asparagus, 46, *47*
    mussel, 54–55, *55*
    potato, Alsatian, *116,* 117
greens, in four-greens tart, 34–35, *35*
green tea, rice pudding parfaits with raspberries and
    cream, 156–57, *157*
grilled tuna with rosemary-fennel coulis, 86, *87*
guinea hen casserole with morels, fava beans, and
    fiddlehead ferns, 96, *97*

H

ham, speck, and sage boules, 124–25, *125*
hamburger, classic, and three variations, 92–93, *93*
herb and rice salad, 84–85
hors d'oeuvres. *See* starters and small bites

I

ice creams, chocolate, trio of, 144–45, *145*
Indian burger, 93

K

kiwi pâtes de fruits, *154, 155*

L

lamb:
    cassoulet, Daniel's casual, *94, 95*
    chops, marinated, with two sauces, 110–11, *111*
    stew with rosemary and orange, *98, 99*
latkes, potato, with smoked salmon, quail eggs,
    and watercress, 26, *27*
lemon:
    cupcakes with mixed berries and ricotta cream,
      165, 166
    Meyer, eggplant-wrapped swordfish with tomato
      and, *72, 73*
    tomato tart, Mediterranean, 30–31, *31*
lemongrass shrimp, melon salad with, *40, 41*
lime, yogurt, and rhubarb dressing, 120
lobster roll sandwich, 80–81, *81*

M

mascarpone cream, 164, *165*
meat and poultry entrées, 91–115
    cassoulet, Daniel's casual, *94, 95*
    chicken, roasted, with grapes, artichokes,
      and a chicory salad, 112–13, *113*
    côte de boeuf, peppered, with pommes
      Pont Neuf and watercress salad, 106–7, *107*
    duck à l'orange, *108, 109*
    guinea hen casserole with morels, fava beans,
      and fiddlehead ferns, *96, 97*
    hamburger, classic, and three variations, 92–93,
      93

lamb chops, marinated, with two sauces, 110–11,
    111
lamb stew with rosemary and orange, *98, 99*
pork, seed-crusted rack of, with cabbage-
    cranberry compote, 100–101, *101*
pork tenderloin, peanut-crusted, with Southern-
    style vegetables, *102,* 102–3
turkey breast, roasted, with endive, apple,
    and walnuts, 104, *105*
venison, roasted, with date sauce and root
    vegetables, 114–15, *115*
Mediterranean tomato-lemon tart, 30–31, *31*
melon salad with lemongrass shrimp, *40, 41*
milk-chocolate ice cream, spiced, 144, *145*
mini baguettes, 128, *129*
mint:
    berrini, 12, *13*
    mojito, Daniel's, 16, *17*
mocha ganache, 164, *165*
mojito, Daniel's, 16, *17*
morels:
    guinea hen casserole with fava beans, fiddlehead
      ferns and, *96, 97*
    penne with spring peas, bacon, eggs and, *56, 57*
mousse, chocolate, *150, 151*
mushrooms:
    chanterelles, stuffed artichokes with Dungeness
      crab and, 42–43, *43*
    morels, guinea hen casserole with fava beans,
      fiddlehead ferns and, *96, 97*
    morels, penne with spring peas, bacon, eggs and,
      56, 57
    porcini, creamy polenta with Parmesan, oregano
      and, 121
mussel(s):
    seafood à l'Orientale, *78, 79*
    stuffed skate with potatoes, saffron butter and,
      66, 67
    velouté, saffron-infused, with mussels gratins,
      54–55, *55*

N

Niçoise lobster pressed sandwich, 81
North African burger, 92–93
nut(s). *See also specific nuts*
    caramel, chocolate cakes with, *142*, 143
    mixed-, cupcakes with Grand Marnier cream,
        165, 167

O

okra, in Southern-style vegetables, *102*, 102–3
olive-crushed potatoes, *70*, 71
orange:
    chamonix à l'orange, *132*, 133
    duck à l'orange, *108*, 109
    glazed sea bream with tomato, pesto and fennel,
        88, *89*
    lamb stew with rosemary and, *98*, 99
    rosemary chocolate ice cream, 145, *145*

P

panna cotta, squash, with cranberry compote and
    walnut tuiles, *162*, 162–63
parfaits, rice pudding, with raspberries and green-
    tea cream, 156–57, *157*
Parmesan:
    baskets with herbed goat cheese, 18, *19*
    creamy polenta with porcini, oregano and, 121
passion fruit:
    soufflés with caramelized pear-passion sauce,
        146, 147
    white-chocolate ice cream, 144, *145*
pâtes de fruits, kiwi, *154*, 155
peanut:
    -crusted pork tenderloin with Southern-style
        vegetables, *102*, 102–3
    sauce, spicy, *36*, 37
pear, caramelized, passion sauce, *146*, 147
peas, spring, penne with morels, bacon, eggs and,
    56, 57
pecans, spiced, in Waldorf moderne, *48*, 48–49
penne with morels, spring peas, bacon, and eggs,
    56, 57
peppered côte de boeuf with pommes Pont Neuf

and watercress salad, 106–7, *107*
pesto, orange-glazed sea bream with tomato,
    fennel and, 88, *89*
phyllo apple tart with Calvados crème anglaise,
    136–37, *137*
pineapple:
    and coconut givré, 140–41, *141*
    gelée, in Waldorf moderne, *48*, 48–49
pistachio and chocolate crêpes suzette, 152–53, *153*
polenta, creamy, with porcini, Parmesan, and
    oregano, 121
pommes Pont Neuf, 106, *107*
porcini, creamy polenta with Parmesan, oregano
    and, 121
pork:
    seed-crusted rack of, with cabbage-cranberry
        compote, 100–101, *101*
    tenderloin, peanut-crusted, with Southern-style
        vegetables, *102*, 102–3
potato(es):
    clam, and tuna marinière, 76, *77*
    gratin, Alsatian, *116*, 117
    latkes with smoked salmon, quail eggs, and
        watercress, 26, *27*
    new, in spring root-vegetable potage with sorrel,
        52, 53
    olive-crushed, *70*, 71
    pommes Pont Neuf, 106, *107*
    and Reblochon tart, 28–29, *29*
    stuffed skate with mussels, saffron butter and,
        66, *67*
pots de crème, chocolate-rum, with cinnamon
    sacristains, 130, *131*
poultry. *See* meat and poultry entrées
pound cake, chocolate-ginger, *138*, 139
pudding(s):
    chocolate bread, with dried fruit, 134, *135*
    rice, parfaits with raspberries and green-tea
        cream, 156–57, *157*

Q

quail eggs, potato latkes with smoked salmon,
    watercress and, 26, *27*

R

radicchio and artichoke clafoutis, *44, 45*
radishes:
    curried tuna-stuffed, 22, 23
    spring root-vegetable potage with sorrel, *52, 53*
raspberries, rice pudding parfaits with green-tea
        cream and, 156–57, *157*
Reblochon and potato tart, 28–29, *29*
red snapper, steamed, in bamboo leaves, 84–85, *85*
rhubarb, yogurt, and lime dressing, 120
rice:
    asparagus and shrimp risotto, 58, *59*
    and herb salad, 84–85
    pudding parfaits with raspberries and green-tea
        cream, 156–57, *157*
ricotta cream, *165*, 166
risotto, asparagus and shrimp, 58, *59*
root vegetable(s):
    potage with sorrel, spring, *52, 53*
    roasted venison with date sauce and, 114–15, *115*
rosemary:
    fennel coulis, grilled tuna with, 86, *87*
    lamb stew with orange and, 98, *99*
    orange chocolate ice cream, *145, 145*
rum:
    chocolate pots de crème with cinnamon
        sacristains, 130, *131*
    mojito, Daniel's, 16, *17*

S

sacristains, cinnamon, 130, *131*
saffron:
    butter, stuffed skate with mussels, potatoes and,
        66, *67*
    -infused mussel velouté with mussels gratins,
        54–55, *55*
sage and speck ham boules, 124–25, *125*
salads:
    carrot-coriander, 33
    chicory, 112–13, *113*
    crispy, 110, *111*
    melon, with lemongrass shrimp, *40*, 41
    rice and herb, 84–85

    Waldorf moderne, *48*, 48–49
    watercress, 106, *107*
salmon, smoked, potato latkes with quail eggs,
        watercress and, 26, *27*
sandwich(es):
    buns, *126, 127*
    hamburger, classic, and three variations, 92–93, *93*
    lobster roll, 80–81, *81*
satay, chicken, with spicy peanut sauce, 36, *37*
sauces:
    Calvados crème anglaise, 136, *137*
    caramelized pear-passion, *146*, 147
    date, 114, *115*
    gingered-tomato, 110, *111*
    goat cheese, 82, *83*
    peanut, spicy, 36, *37*
    raspberries, 156, *157*
    rosemary-fennel coulis, 86, *87*
    spiced-yogurt, 110, *111*
sausages, in Daniel's casual cassoulet, *94*, 95
scallops, caramelized bay, with clementines and
        cauliflower, 62, *63*
sea bass with olive-crushed potatoes, spicy, 70, *71*
sea bream, orange-glazed, with tomato, pesto and
        fennel, 88, *89*
seabreeze, frozen, 16, *17*
shellfish. *See* fish and shellfish entrées
shrimp:
    and asparagus risotto, 58, *59*
    cakes with goat-cheese sauce, 82, *83*
    lemongrass, melon salad with, *40*, 41
side dishes:
    butternut squash gratin, 120
    cabbage-cranberry compote, 100, *101*
    chicory salad, 112–13, *113*
    crispy salad, 110, *111*
    olive-crushed potatoes, 70, *71*
    polenta, creamy, with porcini, Parmesan, and
        oregano, 121
    pommes Pont Neuf, 106, *107*
    potato gratin, Alsatian, *116*, 117
    rice and herb salad, 84–85
    Southern-style vegetables, *102*, 102–3

spaghetti squash with sage, 118, *119*
watercress salad, 106, *107*
yogurt, rhubarb, and lime dressing, 120
skate, stuffed, with mussels, potatoes, and saffron
    butter, 66, *67*
small bites. *See* starters and small bites
soft shell crabs with sorrel cream, *64*, 65
sorrel:
    cream, soft shell crabs with, *64*, 65
    spring root-vegetable potage with, *52*, 53
soufflés:
    passion fruit, with caramelized pear-passion
        sauce, *146*, 147
    strawberry, frozen, 148, *149*
soups:
    beef borscht, spiced, 50, *51*
    chocolate, spiced, with caramel whipped cream,
        158, 159
    root-vegetable potage with sorrel, spring, *52*, 53
    saffron-infused mussel velouté with mussels
        gratins, 54–55, *55*
Southern-style vegetables, *102*, 102–3
spaghetti squash with sage, 118, *119*
spinach, in four-greens tart, 34–35, *35*
spring rolls, crab, Vietnamese, *74*, 75
spring root-vegetable potage with sorrel, *52*, 53
squash:
    butternut, gratin, 120
    panna cotta with cranberry compote and walnut
        tuiles, *162*, 162–63
    spaghetti, with sage, 118, *119*
squid, in seafood à l'Orientale, *78*, 79
starters and small bites, 18–59
    artichoke and radicchio clafoutis, *44*, 45
    artichokes, stuffed, with Dungeness crab and
        chanterelles, 42–43, *43*
    asparagus and shrimp risotto, 58, *59*
    asparagus four ways (steamed, pan roasted,
        gratinéed, and tempura), 46–47, *47*
    beef borscht, spiced, 50, *51*
    blini with caviar and crème fraîche, *24*, 25
    carrot mirror tart with carrot-coriander cream,
        32, 32–33

chicken satay with spicy peanut sauce, *36*, 37
clams, baked littleneck, with prosciutto, *20*, 21
curried tuna-stuffed radishes, *22*, 23
four-greens tart, 34–35, *35*
melon salad with lemongrass shrimp, *40*, 41
mussel velouté, saffron-infused, with mussels
    gratins, 54–55, *55*
Parmesan baskets with herbed goat cheese, 18, *19*
penne with morels, spring peas, bacon, and eggs,
    56, 57
potato and Reblochon tart, 28–29, *29*
potato latkes with smoked salmon, quail eggs, and
    watercress, 26, *27*
root-vegetable potage with sorrel, spring, *52*, 53
tomatoes, Catalan stuffed, 38, *39*
tomato-lemon tart, Mediterranean, 30–31, *31*
Waldorf moderne, *48*, 48–49
stew, lamb, with rosemary and orange, 98, *99*
strawberry(ies):
    berrini, 12, *13*
    soufflés, frozen, 148, *149*
sweet potatoes, in Southern-style vegetables, *102*,
    102–3
swordfish, eggplant-wrapped, with tomato and
    Meyer lemon, 72, *73*

T

tart(s):
    carrot mirror, with carrot-coriander cream, *32*,
        32–33
    four-greens, 34–35, *35*
    phyllo apple, with Calvados crème anglaise,
        136–37, *137*
    potato and Reblochon, 28–29, *29*
    tomato-lemon, Mediterranean, 30–31, *31*
tempura, asparagus, 47, *47*
tomato(es):
    eggplant-wrapped swordfish with Meyer lemon
        and, 72, *73*
    lemon tart, Mediterranean, 30–31, *31*
    orange-glazed sea bream with pesto, fennel and,
        88, *89*
    sauce, gingered, 110, *111*

stuffed, Catalan, 38, *39*
tuiles, walnut, *162,* 162–63
tuna:
    clam, and potato marinière, 76, *77*
    curried, -radishes, 22, *23*
    grilled, with rosemary-fennel coulis, 86, *87*
turkey breast, roasted, with endive, apple, and
        walnuts, 104, *105*
turnips, in spring root-vegetable potage with sorrel,
        52, 53

V

venison, roasted, with date sauce and root
        vegetables, 114–15, *115*
Vietnamese crab spring rolls, *74, 75*
vodka, in frozen seabreeze, 16, *17*

W

Waldorf moderne, *48,* 48–49
walnut(s):
    roasted turkey breast with endive, apple and, 104,
        105
    tuiles, *162,* 162–63
watercress:
    four-greens tart, 34–35, *35*
    potato latkes with smoked salmon, quail eggs and,
        26, *27*
    salad, 106, *107*
white-chocolate passion-fruit ice cream, 144, *145*
white wine, in berrini, 12, *13*

Y

yogurt:
    rhubarb, and lime dressing, 120
    sauce, spiced, 110, *111*